WORLD THROUGH A STETHOSCOPE

VOLUME 1

DR TEJAS SHELAR

To the relentless healers, the tireless learners, and the compassionate souls who embrace the noble calling of medicine—may your unwavering commitment to healing lives light the way for generations to come.

Contents

Contents

Contents

Contents

Introduction

World through a Stethoscope is an idea, which originated amidst the gone pandemic of COVID. With a simple motto of giving voice to healthcare professionals, unfolding stories, one at a time.

With **74 established authors** - who are healthcare professionals, have enlived the text within these pages. They have unveiled the triumphs and challenges, the moments of vulnerability and resilience, that have shaped them as they navigate the maze of healthcare.

In the vast realm of medicine, where every heartbeat holds a story, we find ourselves at the crossroads of science and humanity. Welcome to this anthology, a tapestry woven by the hands, minds, and hearts of medical professionals.

Get ready for an amazing journey! This book is like a collection of stories, put together by people who spend their lives making others feel better. **The narratives in this book are frozen in time, representing the authors as they were around December 2020. However, as we fast forward to 2023, their subsequent achievements and personal growth have taken them to new heights, making their stories even more inspiring and emblematic of their remarkable journeys.**

We hope this book encourages future doctors, makes people talk about how to make things better, and reminds everyone that being a doctor is not just about facts and figures, it's also about being caring and kind. Let's celebrate the special people who spend their lives helping others, and let these stories inspire you to do good things too. Wherever we originate, whoever we are, and wherever we may be headed, our lives are woven from stories, and it's stories that will endure as our lasting legacy.

Dr Tejas Shelar

An individual of unquestionable integrity, the trait that sets Dr. Tejas apart is her ability to unlock people's potential to become better. Unmatched dedication being her trademark, Dr Tejas has been awarded multiple accolades for her academic and extracurricular ventures. Being the first doctor in her entire ancestry, she has paved her way with relentless passion for Medicine.

If we were to summarise Dr. Tejas in one statement, it would be only fitting to say that she's not only the Jack of all trades but also, the Master of All. Evident from what her presence has helped WTS achieve already, she's capable of handling every avenue herself right from having social media at her fingertips to having built the structure to managing marketing and global relations with medical professionals in her spare time; all while leading WTS to it's peak.

Incredibly ambitious and driven, Dr Tejas hasn't fallen short in building her impressive persona outside WTS either; From being a COVID Warrior, an artist - exhibiting her art on International Tour, organising various healthcare camps, to grabbing 8 distinctions in her MBBS, to being awarded the: "Champions of Champions Award" on National level for engaging in impactful community service along with excelling at her academics, amongst 36 other awards, there's little Dr Tejas hasn't dabbled in yet.

She believes, "Leadership is not about the next election, it's about the next generation. I strongly believe that the next generation has the capacity to translate vision into reality. We are the new generation of Healthcare professionals. We are the next."

CHAPTER 1

A Med Student's Gambit: Battling the Pandemic and Finding Purpose

"Even if something bad happens to you, I'll be a proud father knowing that you succumbed on the battlefield, saving lives" said my father to a profusely crying 20-year-old me, stood at the precipice of an unknown world, of this invincible organism, called the COVID-19 virus, while he dropped me at the dreadfully silent hostel campus. The country had sealed itself off from the outside world, while horrible videos dominated the internet. Pandemic, a word whose meaning I had just understood last year, during 2nd year MBBS, was declared. I could never have imagined living through one, let alone volunteering as a healthcare provider, aiding others in navigating this uncharted territory.

March 2020, last week, 21 days lockdown was announced. There was a sudden need for medical professionals to manage the ordeal. Orders were sent across, for recruitment, a voluntary endeavor for those willing to step into the breach. By the first week of April, we had received our instructions. Many of my colleagues' parents had wisely chosen to keep their children safe from harm, a natural response in such perilous times. When I relayed the notice to my parents, my father's response was in stark contrast. He greeted the news with unbridled enthusiasm, proclaiming, *"This is amazing. You're getting a chance to serve your country. You're going."* I admit, it was confusing at first, but an air of excitement began to permeate my thoughts. The prospect of avoiding the monotony of lockdown grew increasingly appealing. My father, a police officer himself, continued his dedicated service throughout this period, and I often went to bed with worry gnawing at my heart for his safety.

He arranged the necessary travel passes for our journey, knowing it was the only means of transportation. He loaded my luggage, provisions, and essentials into the vehicle. We bid heartfelt farewells to my mother and younger brother, and then embarked on our journey. I was filled with anticipation and determination, my earlier trepidation temporarily eclipsed. As we set off, my father informed us of a brief detour to visit a close friend of his. My dad proudly told him about my ordeal. While we were about to leave, he said something that utterly shook me, and gave a reality check.

"Incase, anything ever happens to me, he'll take care of things, I've arranged for everything you'll need until you and Omkar(younger brother) stand on your feet." And that's when I realised the gamble of life I was getting into, and the one my dad was already playing. I burst into tears. Regretting my decision, wanting to go back to the safe walls of home.

My dad, patiently explained,

"Tejas, this is not easy. For anyone. This situation is something we've never experienced in the past, and probably remain so in the annals of history. You're going to be a doctor, it's been your passion since time immemorial, and in trying times, if you run away, would you be able to face your conscience. Even if something bad happens to you, I'll be a proud father knowing that you succumbed on the battlefield, saving lives. Trust me, you'll thank me later."

Sobbing, I gathered myself together. It made sense. Everything flashed before my eyes, the days I'd dreamed about donning the apron, getting into med school, being on the other side of the operating room table as a surgeon.

Well medicine was something I've always wanted to pursue. My orthopaedic surgeon used to joke about my affinity for medicine stemming from my frequent hospital visits as a child, a jest I couldn't deny. . Being operated upon for 7 surgeries, while growing up, I had grown resilient to the fears that gripped others, to the point that I used to promise myself, I had once vowed never to shed a tear during an I.V. cannulation before a surgery. That story, however, was for another time. I eventually grew more curious to how fascinating the world of medicine was. The impact it has. Making a difference in one's life, directly influences the trajectory of families. In a good way. Maybe it might've been the reason for choosing this field.

I wiped my tears, donned a smile and with a lot of hesitation, but found a new found meaning, I decided to go play against the odds.

Next 6 months were the most challenging and beautiful in their own way. Witnessed death, experienced fear, faced the invisible virus, saw remorse, but also, understood the true meaning of resilience and hope.Yet, in the face of uncertainty, I also discovered the true essence of resilience and hope. Uncertainty may be an ever-present companion, but it is our human spirit that empowers us to overcome it. We emerge from each trial stronger than before.

In the end, guess what, at this gamble of life, we won!

"In the grand casino of life, every decision is a roll of the dice. Whether we win or lose, it's the courage to play that defines our

journey."

The pandemic gave birth to "World through a Stethoscope". I developed unwavering patriotism for my field and fellow colleagues.

I'd like to end with one of my favourite quotes, *"You're never ready for what you have to do. You just have to do it. That makes you ready".*

Sarah Ansari

Sarah Ansari is currently an intern in Rajiv Gandhi Medical College, Thane. She has dreamt of becoming a part of the medical community since 8th standard. Like most other students, she has grown in every aspect throughout this journey.

She likes to sink in daydreams while the sea breeze touches her face. When she is not in the hospital you can find her trying out new food places with her friends. She loves to play the ukulele. Capturing sunsets is like therapy to her. She is a warm hug for anyone who needs it.

CHAPTER 2

Processing Death

As an intern I've realized how this is the most beautiful period of our career as a doctor. We are basically walking down a bridge towards the real practice of healthcare. Despite the overwhelming workload and long hours, it is the golden period where we are so close to the patients and learn the most. It gives immense joy and satisfaction to observe the process of healing and the results of it. It feels like a privilege to have people trust in you at their worst times and to see them regain their health.

Being on the field gives a reality check of the situation of our healthcare system. Apart from lack of physical maintenance, our doctors are more exposed to experiences that can take a toll on one's mental health. They witness too much suffering and death on a daily basis. You will have 10 patients discharged in a healthy state but an unfortunate patient will be the one that occupies your mind till the end of the day.

My first encounter with death as a doctor was in the Medicine ward. We had a 65 year old male patient in cardiogenic shock. I was beside the patient, monitoring him in his last few hours, hoping for the increased doses of inotropes to work but his heart gave up and I had to call it. After reporting to the resident, I counselled the family and it was painful to watch them lose their father. This heart- wrenching experience triggered a bundle of emotions in me.

Soon after this I was in my Paediatrics posting. The paediatric ward is the one place I expected to witness a sign of many little humans' perkiness, but instead the the cries of children in pain turned it into a depressive epsiode for me. I remember one night we had all beds in the PICU occupied. Amongst them 4 patients were on ventilator support. It was a matter of few hours till we had 2 of them with dropping levels of oxygen saturation. Despite our best efforts, one of them couldn't make it. The sight of a child's life being cut short before it even begins is simply heartbreaking. The pain that the parents and loved ones go through is unbearable. Every death I witnessed, especially in this ward, was emotionally devastating.

Doctors are often burdened with work and responsibilities, leaving little time to process a patient's death. We have to switch gears quickly and focus on the next patient who needs care. This constant exposure to human suffering can be desensitizing, making it harder to process our feelings. We become numb to the pain and sadness that surrounds us, and it takes a significant emotional toll on us. We have to compartmentalize our emotions while maintaining balance with our professional responsibilities, which can be challenging. There is no direct solution for this complex encounter. As a doctor my method of coping to this harshness is journaling the incident. I prefer to pen down all my emotions that are weighing me down. Talking to loved ones always helps. Different strategies may work for different individuals. All of us should give ourselves the time and space to process every experience and try to be more kind and empathetic to our colleagues, recognizing the emotional burden we carry in our profession. To conclude, I'd like to share something I read- we are all like waves hitting the shore-even after the wave dies it is still a part of the ocean.

Srushti Devgire

Srushti Devgire , is a Third year BPTh Student at Seth GS Medical College and KEM Hosital, Mumbai. She is a hobbyist photographer who loves capture moments and sunsets and a novice ukulele player. She loves travelling and exploring places and learning about it. She is a coffee enthusiast loves to experiment with it.

CHAPTER 3

Finding Hope at Rock Bottom: A Story of Forgiveness and Acceptance

Amidst all of these amazing success stories here, I will tell you my story of failure, or rather survival.

It all started when I enrolled myself for medical entrance exam coaching in 11th grade back in 2016, but I wasn't really sure about my career choices then. I wanted to become a pilot or a doctor, and a lot of other professions caught my interest too, but I was unsure of where my passion lay. I didn't know then that I was in for the long haul when it came to medicine.

Finally, I decided to take a gap year and prepare for NEET properly. Due to my mistakes or at times due to inevitable circumstances, I flunked NEET three times (actually four, but I don't count the first one) really badly. In my last attempt, everything was going swimmingly, and even my teachers were hoping for the best result, but the exam kept being postponed due to COVID. I think I lost my tempo and got saturated. In the last month, my revision was hampered, and the experience of earlier failures used to give me anxiety, as the exam day came closer, and what I feared the most happened. All the efforts I had put in that whole year felt useless as I walked back from the exam center.

All I could think was that I was incapable and couldn't do anything to make this right . I felt very hopeless, hapless, defeated, and lost. Even before the results were out, I knew how terribly I had performed due to the pressure and my anxiety. After the results were out, my parents were obviously disappointed. I can admit now that I felt helpless, even suicidal, as if there was no way out now. My parents, both being very successful academically, I felt they were suffering publicly the ignominy of my defeat. But fortunately, even after all of this, my parents stood by me throughout, and I think that helped me to survive. My chemistry teacher, Naidu Sir, my parents, and some of my friends helped me feel better or less worse. When we checked the counseling brochure, I saw the BPTh course at SETH GS MEDICAL COLLEGE & KEM HOSPITAL. I saw the previous year's cut-off, and it matched up to my score. My Aai said, "Your end goal is to become a doctor and help patients. Even this profession would give you that opportunity to make a difference in someone's life."All I want is to do enough in life so that I can be sure that my Aai is proud of me.Obviously, her words got me thinking, and despite my confusion, I

went ahead and applied for this and got into the physiotherapy course at KEM.

I arrived at college with a lot of regrets and emotional baggage that I knew I had to resolve gradually. I started forgiving myself one day at a time. I spent most of my time in denial, and did things in an attempt to escape reality. Even this brought me new and interesting experiences like exploring and roaming around Mumbai, going to watch sunsets, and visiting coffee places alone. Seemingly, nothing was wrong, but I was more isolated than ever. I felt everyone had figured out the puzzle which I had even failed to understand. As if I was flowing down into an abyss endlessly without any sense of direction, oscillating between thinking I didn't get what I deserved to thinking I don't even deserve what I got. The feeling of not understanding still ,what my purpose is frustrating me to no end.

But things started feeling different from 2nd year. I made friends in college, and started socialising a bit more. All my friends are around 3 years younger than me, but they inspired me to see things differently. My best friend is always one call away here in Mumbai. After my 2nd year results were out, I had an epiphany. It's been two years into this degree and it's high time I forgive myself completely and move ahead. If not now, never. I decided to let time show what it had to offer me, and from my side, I would only try to give my best. For the first time, I felt I had accepted my reality, and acceptance felt like freedom from years of imprisonment, but it took very long to get there. I understand my mistakes, and I still carry my regrets, but I feel they are way lighter on my back now. I am still learning, and I have mentally reached a place that seemed really far a few months ago. Also, as a medical student during postings, you come across some patients, and then you can't help but reflect that if this person has the strength to be hopeful, why can't I think a bit differently? With time, I have come to realise the potential and possibilities of this profession to create a difference in someone's life.

I think my story is not a conventional story of success. It's a story about finding a little hope at rock bottom and forgiving yourself. My dad once said, "Sometimes you don't choose the profession; the profession chooses you." I just hope his words will be proved right in the coming years, just like catching the wrong train but reaching the desired destination.

Dr. Dipti Bhagat

Dr. Dipti Chetan Bhagat has done M.B.B.S in 1996 from Government Medical College, Surat. She has done M.D. Paediatrics in 1999 from Government Medical College, Surat. She had prepared a Patient guidance booklet on T.B and Diabetes under guidance of a senior doctor during her internship She had worked as Resident Doctor in Lilavati Hospital and Research Center. She is doing her private practice as consultant at 'Kshiltij Clinic' at Matunga, Mumbai. She had done PALS (Paediatric Advanced Life Support) course. She had been offering her medical knowledge of school kids whenever required ! She is a life member of IAP (India Academy of Paediatrics and IMA (India Medical Association)

CHAPTER 4

Being a Doctor

Going down memory lane, I remember when I realized that my ambition was to become a Doctor. Although my parents were not from the medical profession, my grandfather and many uncles, who were close to me, were a part of this noble profession. Having grown up in an environment full of doctors, my goal to become a doctor was crystal clear. As a small-town girl from Gujarat with a vernacular background, I was ready to put in the extra efforts to qualify as a doctor.

My first day at the medical college started with an anatomy lecture where we assembled at the dissection hall. Our professor briefed us about being a doctor. The medical profession is not as glamorous as you see on the screen is what our professor began with, since he had seen some of the students with buttons of their apron open- a trend in movies only. In reality, a doctor had to have the buttons of their aprons fully closed. Adhering to this protocol, to date I have the buttons of my apron closed completely. My passion for the profession made the physiology practicals memorable as we were taught to measure basics such as the pulse, blood pressure and physical examination.

I tried to master medical knowledge to the best of my ability. By the end of the MBBS course, I had practically gone through all the disciplines of the science, including Ophthalmology, orthopedics, ENT, skin, surgery, medicine, Obstetrics & Gynecology and of course, my favorite- Pediatrics, during the clinical posting. The exposure to various disciplines enabled me to decide that I am cut out for Pediatrics - which I enjoyed the most.

Next was the one-year internship, which was coupled with the excitement of becoming a full-fledged doctor and hence, brought out the best in me. It consisted of three months of rotationary posting at the primary health center with a fortnight of exposure to each of the departments. From our exposure to some of the villages whose names were Latin and Greek to us, to handling patients all by ourselves for the first-time, to being a part of the pulse polio programs, all were unforgettable and highly-knowledgeable experiences.

According to the flow of the system, we had to give 3 preferences for our postgraduate course, however, being extremely passionate and clear about likings, I filled in only one option, which was pediatrics. I was lucky enough that blessings and my hard work paid off as I got into my dream branch.

During my residency days, the Pediatric ward became my whole world. Each experience during those days was learning in itself. We had to be alert the entire time and run without thinking twice for a labor call as soon as the bell rang. Furthermore, we had to be available 24/7 for patients and also had to study for our upcoming exams. This is exactly parallel to how a doctor's life is once they start their practice, the only difference being the doctor's need to keep updated by conferences and reading, not for their exams, but the betterment of the patients and the society. Hence, those days really acted as a simulation and showed me the amount of dedication one requires to be a doctor. The rounds with the professors during those days were the main pillars, since the discussions during rounds were a treasure of knowledge. The small celebrations in the ward after the first time successfully completing procedures like lumbar puncture, intubation and exchange transfusion are still memorable. T.B OPD, vaccination day, case presentation day, working on Dissertation, etc. became an integral part of the residency days.

At the end of 8 years of rigorous work, I received the prestigious post of Pediatrician, ready to practice with utmost confidence and enthusiasm.

I believe in a few principles based on the things I learned during the journey to becoming a doctor. The first one being- a doctor's knowledge is a continuous process with technology and research constantly upgrading the medical field. On top of that, with each case, there is something new to learn which should be implemented thereafter. Followed by, strictly using only authentic medical sources to be updated. And the final one being never overlooking the basics as there are no shortcuts where a human life is involved.

After becoming a mother, I could put myself in a patient's shoes, easily. This helped me know the right way in which I could relieve the anxiety within the parents of my patients.

There is a vast difference in the medical field in the twenty years since I have started my practice. For instance, there have been many new vaccines that have been introduced along with an increase in the incorporation of artificial intelligence in the medical field. However, something which will never change is that I enjoy being a doctor and seeing a patient recover gives me happiness and peace.

Dr. Zeal Mithani

Dr. Zeal Mithani is a young professional pursuing her internship at MGM Medical College, Navi Mumbai. People describe her as an epitome of exuberant energy radiating bliss all around.

She is meticulous and bagged a Top 2 rank with 10 distinctions throughout her MBBS.

One of her major qualities is leadership & working with logical convictions at the different posts. Amongst them are two well known International organizations, she was the Professional Development Director & Co-founder of Rotaract Club of Medicrew and the National Student Research Council Coordinator at Global Consortium Of Medical Education & Research.

She feels immense joy to have conducted a PAN-India Health camp for Orphans in tough times during the Pandemic .She loves to swim her way through the depth of Oceans by her work and strives to inspire and learn from people.

CHAPTER 5

Striving towards my Medi-Goal

Do you ever think that dreams are deceptive? Wonder what that thin line between dreams and reality is? It's the efforts and vision that takes to turn those dreams into reality. In my childhood, I had been naive about the importance of ambitions and success. But one thing that was crystal clear and stamped in my mind like an unbroken seal was that I will become a Doctor. Maybe at that point, it was the feeling of being the *first to-be Doctor* of my family or the pride I would see in my mother's eye?

Well, it all fell in place when I realized that the white coat kept pulling me towards it like a magnet turning my dreams into reality. And the midnight oil I am burning on my journey of becoming a doctor has become an integral part of my circadian rhythm.

From my first day at med school to the end of my first year, it has been a roller coaster ride. The admission process was very stressful, thinking that my marks would get me admission easily in a private medical college, being unfortunate as the cut off for that year shot way too high and the only option left for me was to get enrolled in a deemed university, in which I currently study. Hence my admission got delayed till the MopUp Round 1- which delayed my first year of college by a month. At first, the stress infiltrated my mind with a lot of pessimistic thoughts but as I went to my college for admission, my outlook towards it changed on seeing my huge college campus with a hospital with an endless patient incoming.

Experiencing a burst of mixed emotions on the first day of college with a whole new set of unknown faces could have been petrifying, but Med school is an amazing place to be. Stepping into the Dissection Hall for the first time and taking the Oath as I held the scalpel in my hand, I felt like I have the skills and sharpness of a Surgeon already. As we dissected the body and removed different organs to study them, I felt grateful for the dead who are teaching the living, immortalizing themselves in our memory as we clear our basics and learn Anatomy.

Understanding the difference between the feel of a blood vessel and nerve for the first time to the time when we cut open the skull to remove the brain or the time we cut open the rib cage to study the lungs and heart, each experience has a story to tell. But to sum it all up, the feeling of holding the organs in my hands is ineffable to express in mere words. Being the enthusiastic self that I am, I did not want to restrict my learning to the adult human body, hence I grabbed the best opportunity I got at a Fetal Dissection Workshop at DY Patil Hospital. Learning the difference of pressure, we need to apply while dissecting a fetus vs an adult human body completely blew my mind. Truly dissection has become an indelible memory of my first year.

As my first year progressed, the second year brought with it my first clinical exposure as the hospital wards welcomed me with their open arms. Everyday clinical postings seemed so much fun, going around talking to patients, taking their history and examining them. The best part was the look in their eyes which reflected hope to get better and blessings for the one who treats them. So much for the blessings that when I walked through the wards to take the history of other patients, I also kept a check on the older ones. They would call me a Doctor already and ask me to examine and treat them. These things are quite usual when we become practicing doctors but as a medical student, it felt like how a mother's heart beats with joy when her child calls her Maa for the first time.

Sadly, the clinical postings came to an end quite abruptly with the onset of the Pandemic. Virtual case Presentations wouldn't give us that feeling of taking history and communicating with patients. I somewhere kept missing the knowledge that needed to be delivered to the layman and the knowledge I had to seek to flourish as a medico. *God always has the right path planned for you when in dire need of something.*

I got a chance to be a part of two International Medical organizations. Being a part of *Team Professional Development* and co-founding my own Medical Non-Profit organization - *Rotaract Club of Medicrew* at such a young age was the best thing that could've happened to me in this quarantine. This platform opened doors for several ideas I had to improve the community and modernize medical learning.

It also gave me the chance to improve my clinical skills through the several health camps we conducted. *Project H.O.P.E (Helping Orphans Prosper till Eternity)*- how surreal does it sound! A Pan-India Health camporganized and executed by me focused on ameliorating the health of orphans- a sector of society neglected amidst the pandemic. Examining nearly 150 kids with all safety precautions and interacting with them seeing the way their eyes shone brighter than the daylight gave me a great insight into their lives. They were so intrigued by all the medical equipment that they couldn't contain their curiosity and it was so heart-warming to see their elated faces and to assure them that they had someone to care for their health and well-being during the pandemic. This camp will leave its footprints on the sands of time in my medical journey.

Little did I know that I also had a tech geek side to me which came to existence as I successfully designed my very first

Virtual Case Simulationwebsite- simulating each case by using animations and helping the user understand the correct line of treatment.

I have much more to achieve in my medical career, but as each day passes by, I see several opportunities raining over me and I'm ready to grab all the drops to harvest my future. The phase of dreaming to be a doctor is far behind now, I'm now on a path that has no turning back from my Medi-goal. Every day I am striving to be the Doctor my Mother has always envisioned me as!

Devang Srivastava

Devang is a medical student who has an excellent academic record and good standing in his college. He enjoys participating in various activities outside of his curriculum, has numerous research publications, and has been involved in various organizations.

He has a passion for science and has shown this throughout his life by excelling in various activities, including sports, music, literature, debates, and more.

His favorite authors include Yuval Noah Harari, Dr. Joseph Murphy, Harper Lee, V.S. Ramachandran, and James Clear. Devang also loves traveling and taking photographs, and he has a knack for quizzing. He is interested in genetics and neurology, and is keen to pursue a career in one of these fields. He also enjoys volunteering and has organized health camps across the country.

CHAPTER 6

Solution to Dilemma and Boredom in Medicine

Being a science enthusiast, I always liked to do things, be curious about things around me and I had fun doing so. But when I ended up in Medical College, I was unable to understand why I ended up here? What was the reason? Why was my academic life so monotonous?

So now, if you feel the same way, I would like to answer with some of my experiences.

A Reason

I remember my first lecture in college, still a newbie, with no idea what will happen. Suddenly the professor entered the hall and we all stood up to wish her. Then she introduced herself and told us to do the same. Well, that was easy. But then she asked us to tell what inspired us to join the profession? Well, that is also easy- no wait- what was my reason? Love for science? The zeal to do something good for society? To be frank, with these reasons I could have done anything else too. Become a scientist, go for civil service, etc. But Why M.B.B.S.? At that time, I gave a vague answer that I don't remember.

That was the worst dilemma I had ever faced in my life. This struggle continued till the end of my first year. I did learn and enjoyed learning, but that hole remained there. Then we started our clinical postings.

The first one was General Medicine- the one which gave me hope that what I learned in my pre-clinicals was worth it. I learned a lot, (though less than what I expected- no professor cares, you are on your own, brutal reality), thanks to postgraduates and interns who took us a bit seriously. I felt the hole had started to fill up, though I was still unable to know why I ended up where I am.

Then came OBS-GYN. In Gynaecology, I was finally able to understand why I joined medicine. At least that was what I thought. The story goes like this: We were in the Operation Theatre. The case was a C-section due to some abnormal positioning of the fetus. The surgery went well. The baby was out. A just fresh out of anatomy student like me was happy to have successfully identified the layers of the abdominal wall. But then our Professors started talking to each other. I went close to them, the other students also followed. The professors noticed us and told us that the baby was a bit bluish. So, they

kept him in an incubator and then asked us to keep him awake. Then we started touching him, poking his feet with our fingers.

Then suddenly he opened his eyes and *smiled*.

That smile was not just a smile. To me, it was something even more. I felt great and thought that these moments are the ones that make learning and memorizing stuff so useful. Happiness was the new reason that came to mind.

But then surgery posting also mesmerized me. I learned new things and even imagined how cool it would be to save someone from the claws of death. But this feeling was different. I remember that I even said that I joined to support my family members but ever since I started losing the loved ones around me, I think that was a naive reason.

Then I felt that the reasons keep piling up as we mature more.

In the end, I concluded that the reason is an ever-evolving subject.

So, you should not worry if you don't have yours yet. Do whatever you enjoy doing and learn how to balance it with your studies.

But do select your profession with some prior idea about it. Or else it will deviate you from the path that is the best suited for you.

Tinkering with the Molecular Giants: A curiosity - filled research experience

Now let's shift to something a bit more alluring. Research – a necessity in medical science. I think you will agree with this (all hail COVID). But it is not limited to just what you are thinking now.

It is a whole new universe or even a multiverse I was lucky enough to be exposed to, even if it was just a bit of it.

I went to the Centre for Cellular & Molecular Biology, Hyderabad, after getting selected for the Winter Research Observer-ship Programme. I was very excited about my first research experience. The lab I had shown interest in was Virology (a mere coincidence; COVID again). On our first day, I met the Senior Resident Fellow under whom I was supposed to spend more than half of my 12 days of research experience. On the first day itself, I saw many things- Gel Electrophoresis, ELISA, P.C.R., went to visit the animal house, and saw the zebrafish facility. However, I never felt fatigued, due to the excitement. Every night all my fellow observers and I used to gather to discuss what happened in our respective labs and every morning we attended lectures which were very intriguing. Sometimes, we used to ask some fellows to discuss what they do in their labs, even if it took 10 PM to go back to our quarters.

I used to roam around and explore new concepts, like genetics- the Drosophila Lab was one of my favorites. There, we used to discuss fascinating stuff about gene editing in the small flies. We also discussed CRISPR-Cas9, and saw the research on Organoids- which was an intriguing topic. N.M.R. helped me see physics from a new angle. The X-Ray Crystallography of proteins also gave birth to some fascination. Some crazy microscopic images and B.S.L.-2 and 3 visits were also new to me.

Then one evening, we went to LaCONES (Laboratory for the Conservation of Endangered Species), saw leopards and learned about artificial insemination. We attended a lecture on Microfluidic and paper fluidic devices which is a potentially cost-effective method for the diagnosis of pregnancy and other chronic diseases in the coming days.

I had a good time and the experience made my college life mundane-free.

I will also like you to go and attend this in your college life. Never shy from learning something new and make some great memories.

I will like to end my part with a favorite quote:

"Somewhere, something is waiting for you to be known"

Explore new horizons without fearing about the why. If it is meant to happen, it will happen. So put an end to your struggle and enjoy the moment and give your best in whatever you want to achieve.

Chirag Chawla

"We don't live in a universe of rules, we live in a universe of chances."

Chirag is a goofball at heart wrapped up with an exterior of witty sarcastic comments. He is your go-to person when you want to get a task done immaculately.

He is a self-acclaimed multi-tasker who comes with every shade of surprise. He can go from eating pizza and binge watching like a couch potato to a workaholic in seconds.

While the world saw this pandemic and the lockdown as a confining cage, Chirag explored several of his skills and tested the extent of his potential by grabbing every opportunity that came his way.

Chirag loves to travel, explore new places, meet new people and go on adventures. He's recently discovered his passion of biking and long bike rides!

CHAPTER 7

"It Doesn't Need To Be Perfect"

"Everything happens for a reason"

A pretty generic & cliché quote, right? Well, it often turns out to be quite true.

Back in August 2018, I stepped into the premises of Government Medical College, Miraj still trying to grasp the reality of not getting admission in my college of my desire, all the while cursing myself for the black dot mistakes on my OMR sheet that will forever be etched in my memory. Miraj being a dusty town, with dust being my biggest foe as an allergen made me brood more than I already was.

1 month into living in the hostel, I got ill with severe rhino-sinusitis *(Is the author even a medico if there are no medical terms in the book?)*. Following this, I shifted out to an apartment, with the superhero of my life, *my mother*, who decided to come down to live with me and look after my health. The following months were tough, battling my fight with dust & sinusitis, wrapping myself up as the Invisible Man, dodging ice-creams & cold-drinks, and turning stainless-steel glasses yellow with the Turmeric-Salt gargling.

But now that I look back, Miraj had already started sharing various experiences with me, subconsciously helping me learn & grow as a person. Miraj gave me the experience of traveling alone on my own for the first time via a bus from Miraj to Pune & back for the long weekends. Even in a short span of 1

month at the hostel, I got to know people from all the nooks &
corners and even learned to initiate relations with everyone.

My college has a very interesting tradition, or rather a
relationship between seniors & juniors. Being prohibited to
bring our own vehicles in the First Year, all juniors approach
their seniors to borrow vehicles for outings. Whenever seniors
& juniors go out to eat, the bill is always taken care of by the
seniors. There has never been a question there. I further got
to experience the Indian Festivals in their full spectrum, with
huge events being organized during Ganpati, as well as Navratri
along with the Garba Nights. As I approached February 2019,
wherein I single-handedly handled the bookings & registrations
for Trinity, a national level medical conference at LTMMC,
Sion, Mumbai *(The first opportunity I came across unknowingly)*.
Soon we were traveling to different colleges for conferences &
events, exploring different cultures & initiatives. The brooding
phase had slowly started fading.

We move ahead to the honeymoon year of MBBS i.e., 2nd
year which is packed with organizing events for our juniors and
the biggest highlight being a trip to the North, famously known
as "Pulse". By now, my health had improved considerably
and was no longer as heavy a burden as it used to be. As
we fast forward to March 2020, the major chunk of the
honeymoon year is over. Any common 2nd year MBBS student
starts focusing on their academics by this time, after barely
having passed their first terminals. I was following the same
path when suddenly we were hit by the pandemic and
everything was shut down with everyone pushed inside their
houses for an indefinite time.

Honestly speaking, the first few weeks were as fun as it
would've been for any medical student, who could catch up
on their sleep. It was complete bliss. But 1 month into the
lockdown, looking at new emerging trends, events & activities, I

realized how I was uninvolved with regards to extracurriculars. These thoughts carried negative emotions with them, which eventually started hampering my mental health. This is when I realized, the only way out is by working for it, and I simply went for it.

"Because, Why Not?"

I decided to grab all the opportunities that came my way, from WhatsApp forwards of different medical student organizations to Instagram stories. I even started using the email app more often. This came with a very embarrassing backstory (Because I'd created my Email back in 7th Standard. Need I say any more?). I explored various aspects & tested the extent of my skills by saying "Yes" to every opportunity that came my way. It all started writing an article on Geriatric Mental Health, which led me to become the person that I am today. Writing an article made me work towards organizations & earn various positions of responsibilities in different medical student organizations, including State Coordinator of Maharashtra for Rotaract Club of Caduceus as well as The White Coat Project, Unit Member of MSFC India-Unit & Local Exchange Officer in MSAI and many more. My latest achievement being selected in the IFMSA Delegation at the Open Education Conference 2020, a delegation of only 15 members selected from across 124 countries. Additionally, I've also been selected for 3 international medical student exchange programs. From working in different teams to founding the Book Club & a Student Research Council for my own college and leading numerous teams, I've honestly explored more than I ever could. With the help of these different opportunities, I could work on myself & numerous skills, shaping and developing myself.

What I want to convey through this story is that none of this would've happened had I not come to Miraj. Whatever happened, actually did happen for a reason. Even though at times you can't see the reason right before your eyes, it's still there. I wouldn't have gained the experience, knowledge & skills I have today had I not come to Miraj nor if I was not stuck at home in a pandemic.

Miraj was the empty platform that harnessed all my ambitions. The fact that GMC Miraj wasn't active in various co-curricular activities turned out to be my opportunity. I honestly believe I wouldn't be the person I am today if there hadn't been a pandemic or if I hadn't been admitted to GMC Miraj. Above all, I wouldn't have been the person I am today without the biggest support of my life, my mom & dad, Yogini Chawla & Pankaj Chawla. And a special mention to the other supporters in my life, Richa Sinha, and my closest friends, Soham Dhume, Chandrashekhar Singh & Naitik Khandelwal who have helped me throughout my journey.

Harshitha Nandimandalam

I am Harshitha, a 2nd medical student studying in Santhiram medical college in Andhra Pradesh. I am very glad to be a part of this book.Although my medical journey is a combination of FAILURES and SUCCESS, I have enjoyed each and every moment in this journey.Actually we can learn more from failures when compared to success.I really enjoyed my time in postings.My final goal is to become a CARDIOLOGIST in America.

CHAPTER 8

Medical journey in the Past days

I am from a Rural area, where becoming a doctor is a stubborn thing. Now, I am going to share a real incident that inspired me a lot. In the early '90s, a great man from my village secured an MBBS seat. He is none other than my uncle, *Dr.Bhaskar Raju* Garu. He completed his MBBS from a prestigious college, named, *Sri Venkateswara Medical College*, Tirupathi, Andhra Pradesh, India. You all may be thinking that getting a Medical Seat was very easy in those days by doing some hard work. But he came from a very poor family where his mother was working in fields to provide money for his son's coaching fee. At last, he completed his MBBS from SVMC and he decided to go to the United States of America to pursue his further studies. In those days, doing PG in America after completing MBBS in India was very difficult as it included the USMLE process. You know what, USMLE is the toughest exam in the *World*. He studied very hard and finally completed PG in Psychiatry after finishing *USMLE Step-1 and Step-2*. Finally, my Uncle wanted to settle in America itself, so he also completed *USMLE Step -3* to pursue a fellowship in American College. This was a very difficult medical journey for my uncle. He then opened his own Medical Practice in Florida, U.S.A. in 2005. He currently serves as the Medical Director of *Orlando Psychiatric Associates*. Now, he has 3 of his own Hospitals in different parts of America. A medical student's journey from a rural area to owning 3 Hospitals in America is *incredible*. Although the medical journey is very long and hard, in the end, it's quite worth it. From this, we can understand that anything can be achieved in life with determination and dedication towards your passion along with some hard work, no matter what the situation is. The word impossible itself is saying, I am Possible. So, don't worry about the long medical journey, and also don't get jealous of your engineering friends who settled earlier than us. Everyone lives in this world, but not everyone gets an opportunity to save another's life. Only *Doctors* can get that opportunity to save patients' lives. Work hard and achieve your goals.

Dear Medical Students, you don't study to pass the test,

you study to prepare for the day where you are the only thing between a patient and a grave.--Mark Reid

Sanjana Agrawal

Sanjana Agrawal, BDS Intern Pupil on her way to emerge as the primary health practitioner in her entire ancestry. She is acing her academics with qualifications and as a clincher. She has excelled in her academics and even socially dynamic. Sanjana as President is leading the Junior Wing of JCI Nagpur Medico organization in her metropolis.

Sanjana is keen on writing and chasing her dream to become a writer, she is co-author for COVID-19 book for dental scholars and even published her original 4+ research articles in Dental Journals of India. Overall, she has stowed more than 35 honors till now as a Dental Student. She is known as the pony of the race as triumphing is in her blood.

Sanjana's parents say she is the child every parent desires to have. Sanjana believes that self-motivation is the key to success.

CHAPTER 9

My Journey Of Dentistry

I am the first child in my entire ancestry who opted for the medical field. In the Medical field, I selected a Bachelor of Dental Sciences (BDS) in the year 2016. On the first day of my college, I understood that dentistry won't be a simple excursion. However, keeping my soul high, I familiarized myself with all the dental equipment and especially carvings in my very first year.

Easily, I went to my subsequent year and soon realized that the year was brimming with delight and thrilling as we used to be back home in only 3-4 hours of college. On account of this, I lost my interest in studies, but discovered my kick in extracurricular activities. I began doing original research and in the long run won several prizes under the category of poster, paper presentation, and table clinics in dental conferences across India. My incandescently happy day was when my very first article got published in the Indian Journal of Dentistry. Even my research got coverage in the student magazine of the Indian Dental Association (IDA).

After my second-year results were out, I was very vexed and disillusioned with myself as I didn't score to my latent capacity. However, soon I raised my soul of inspiration to incredible stature. I began creating interest in my subjects and simultaneously my inclinations towards research increased and I started handling 2-3 my original researches at a glance. Paper and poster presentations became my everyday normal and consecutively, I brought shrubs. I got the best paper and poster presentation for two back-to-back years.

Dealing with my examinations, original research and a functioning individual from the medical association was difficult for me. However, with God's elegance and with consistent help from my folks, I had the option to oversee it positively. By the end of my third year, two more of my researches got published in Dental Journals of India and I had an extraordinary opportunity to do an investigation, which largely expanded my insight, assurance, and advance toward arriving at my fantasy to turn into an Official Author.

Also, the day when my results were out for the third year it was the most joyful moment as I got Distinction in Oral Pathology and I was the Second Clincher of my Cluster. It was a happy moment for my family, my guide, educators, and seniors.

With incredible eagerness, I began my last year, however gradually my plan got pressed with lectures, patients, week-by-week tests, and other social activities. Not long after 2 months of my last year, I got the greatest open door from the medical association JCI Nagpur Medico to lead the Junior Wing as a President. It was a euphoric moment and I couldn't prevent myself from saying yes to it, regardless of my folks saying I needed to avoid this due to my riotous timetable and studies. At that point, I chose to prioritize my work and effectively dealt with my final year prospectus along with being a Junior President and composing research articles, and presenting papers and posters in dental conferences and sponsorship with grants. Some of the exceptional honors I got during this period were Best All-Rounder Student of Year, Women Achiever Award, Excellence Award in Academics.

As a Junior President, there were numerous obligations and desires from the associations that I needed to satisfy. I had the option to finish with consistent direction and the backing of guardians, seniors, and my team. My endeavors got demonstrated when I got All the Awards under Junior Wing Category under JCI.

The defining moment of my excursion when lockdown occurred...

This period turned into a brilliant time for me as I drew out my possibilities and the genuine me. I had the option to satisfy my fantasies, which had been in my mind for such a long time.

Writing helps me upgrade my insight, imagination, and express my actual internal identity. My first fantasy about becoming an Author began as I finished the 1-month Dental Internship Writing course. As an Author I have written in more than 500 blogs for dental students in relationship with Dental Organization- *Dentowesome*, I have even written for a COVID-19 book for dental students as a Co-Author and now I am writing for one more book as a Co-Author.

My wish came true of getting interviewed, As I got interviewed for "The Other Side of My Life" by Indian Dental Association (IDA) and my interview got published in the student magazine of IDA and the other extraordinary thing that happened was that I got coverage on the cover page of the IDA magazine.

I wanted to share the screen and give talks, which got accomplished with YouTube directly in a joint effort with *Dentowesome*- covering each part of dentistry on the channel.

My speaking aptitudes, certainty expanded to an extraordinary level, I won numerous discourse rivalries and another fantasy about training got satisfied as I took live talks for the dental undergraduates. With this, all my original researches, publications were going in full swing. I have given my final year exams and am energetically hanging tight for the outcomes. At the time I wrote this my results were not yet out.

I feel that extracurricular activities are fundamental as they add endless abilities and assist you with developing as a person. Along these lines, aside from the examinations, everybody ought to have a few extracurricular movements which assist you with keeping your inspiration and soul in statues.

I am the first student in the whole lineage of my college to do research publications and packed countless honors as an undergrad. Till now in my four years of dentistry, I have accomplished 35+ honors, which were conceivable due to the consistent direction, backing, and inspiration of my family, guide, educators, seniors, and companions.

I want to advise every student pursuing this to cherish their field -whatever it is and to make progress, confide in yourself and be your self-inspiration because nobody can rouse you better than yourself. Make the most of your field and existence both absolutely. You need to constantly have confidence in yourself and never prevent yourself from developing.

Muskaan Shah

A newly minted intern dreaming her way into a residency of her choice, Muskaan is an academic with a creative heart. She proves her duality by demonstrating her abilities in both examinations, as well as extracurriculars. Her best feature is her compassion towards all living creatures and her determination to be the successful doctor she wishes to be.

She shows maturity in handling tough situations and has been at the forefront of several events as an Editor for the Student Council from 2020-21. Being an Editor for her college magazine has given her an opportunity to amalgamate her love for literature with her love for medicine. Her creativity and skill in writing and editing, brought opportunity back to her door in the form of the Executive Editor position for this book.

She is a passionate individual who tries her best in all endeavors. In her free time, she enjoys reading, art and wants to write a novel of her own some day.

CHAPTER 10

Spectrum

Dispersion is the phenomenon of splitting of white light into its constituent colors. These colors, visible after white light is passed through a prism, make up the spectrum of visible light. It is that very spectrum that makes up the threads of the apron we wear- those iridescent colors that appear when we put that worn and pallid apron in front of a glass prism.

Violet is for your first step into medical college- the color you see when you start to believe in magic again. The color you see when you open up your anatomy textbook for the very first time and run your fingers along brightly colored diagrams of the very thing you can feel raging against your ribcage. Violet is the color of the bruises on your fingertips after multiple failed attempts to draw enough blood for those hematology practicals. Violet is the result of too much or too little reagent in the biochemistry lab.

Indigo is the color of mistakes. Indigo is the color of doubt creeping into your mind as you fail your first exam. It is the color of the night sky out your window as you sit cramming to do better on the next one. It is the ink that flows out of your pen as you frantically scribble down your answer in the last ten minutes of your final. Indigo is the satisfaction you get when you see that distinction beside the very subject you failed in.

Blue is the first day of second year, the first day of clinical postings. Your steps through the wards leave periwinkle footsteps, your fumbling words as you ask patients their histories come out in wisps of azure- wisps of optimism that ease a little suffering, a little pain. The harsh light of the OT lamps transforms the surgeons' scrubs to a dazzling electric blue. And as you watch, it transforms them- from ordinary men and women, to exemplars who look like they belong between the pages of graphic novels. Blue is the color of the feeling in your chest as you close your eyes that night and know you made the right decision.

The bile you feel rising in your throat while you sit across from your examiner is a bright Green. It is the brief flicker of exhaustion you feel, the last chilly breeze before spring blooms before your eyes. Before the color of life, of nature, envelops you. Green is the color of *growth*. It is the shade you see when you stop fearing those exam scores, when you start seeing your future ahead of you. Green is the agar plate with bacterial colonies growing on them- it is the emerald glint of identifying them correctly.

Yellow is the color of the sun, bearing down on you as you enjoy your college fest. It is the brief reprieve between two rigorous years. It is the gold of competition, of wanting to be first in class. It is the dull ochre of failing to do so and still wanting to try again. The friendships you make are a rich, incandescent honey- sticky and sweet against your tongue, coating your words as they teach you to navigate human relations.

The sky outside the window of your train is awash in shades of orange as you travel for your early morning Medicine lecture. The light in the canteen lights up your breakfast like a bonfire- a meal you hurriedly swallow down as a glance to your watch indicates you are late for your clinical posting again. Orange is the luminous image of the retina in your ophthalmology OPD. It is the burn in your chest after you run up the stairs for your next lecture. Orange is passion for your profession, the steady flame of love, fear and determination.

Red is the pounding in your chest. Red are the splatters on the doctors' scrubs, the thin film covering the neonate. It is the pool by the legs of the woman and the love in her gaze as she smiles at the bundle of cloth and life handed to her. Red is the color of the cross on the ambulance, on the first aid kit, on the entrance of the hospital. It is the color of every milestone you have crossed so far- from the heart you held in first year to the cracked open chest cavity you observe surgeons operating on now. Red is the color of your ambition. Red is the tinge of reality.

White is how the story begins. White is the cape you put on your back, the armor you strap on. It is the oath you take, the promises you make, the role you immerse yourself into because it is one you want to play all your life. The people who inspire you are etched in marble, the wish to make them proud is etched in something less fragile. Your hopes and dreams are pearly- pure intentioned and priceless. White is the color of the sterile sheets in the hospital you will work at one day, you know that day is distant and yet you can almost smell the antiseptic in the air. White is the color of dreams coming true.

Dr. Alhad Mulkalwar

Dr. Alhad Mulkalwar has completed his undergraduate from Seth GSMC and KEM Hospital, Mumbai. He has been interested in Medical Research and Innovation, with a total of 10 original research articles and 10 case reports in reputed medical journals. He has won 7 awards for best research paper/poster presentation and 6 awards for best symposium at various National and International Medical Conferences. Alhad has also been an avid quizzer, having won 13 national and international quizzen in the subjects of Physiology, Community medicine, Orthopedics, Psychiatry, Plastic Surgery and Dermatology. He has been awarded numerous recognitions and scholarships for his outstanding contribution to the field of Medical Research and Education. He has been credited as the founder of KEMP's student run organization for promotion and support of Research and Innovation – A.S.P.I.R.E. He wishes to become an Indian Foreign Service officer and is currently preparing for the same

CHAPTER 11

The Path Less Traveled

"This is what we should have thought of years ago! " remarked a senior professor at the Annual General Body Meeting 2019-20. The motion passed with an overwhelming majority and A.S.P.I.R.E. was now formally a part of the glorious twin institutes of Seth G.S. Medical College and King Edward Memorial Hospital, Mumbai.

The journey of this small endeavor was merely one of many enriching experiences I have witnessed throughout M.B.B.S. Well, they could have simply named the course B.M.B.S for Bachelor of Medicine, Bachelor of Surgery but they chose *'Medicinae Baccalaureus Baccalaureus Chirurgiae.'* It does make sense now; why would such a uniquely extravagant course deserve a simple and straightforward name?

I am barely able to recollect the shy and introverted me who started this rollercoaster ride with the only ambition of becoming a decent doctor someday. Necessity is the mother of invention, and rightfully so, a city like Mumbai and a college like GSMC did demand smartness, a quality I wasn't much familiar with before. This place had an uncanny vibe as if telling us that it was much more than just a degree it offered, a world full of unexplored avenues and untapped resources eagerly waiting to be exploited. Rather than setting up new barriers to overcome; it revealed my very own self-imposed barriers to which I would often be a helpless victim.

I have spent the better part of my childhood being an ideal student, consciously avoiding mistakes and failures, a perfect recipe for a spotless, impeccable profile. The education system focuses much on being careful not to fall. But this raised a genuine doubt: Was bypassing the rough patches actually conducive to my development or was it instead counterproductive?

'Some failure in life is inevitable. It is impossible to live without failing at something. Unless you have lived cautiously, you might not have failed at all, but in which case, you might have failed by default.'

-JK Rowling.

We would do our future generations a much greater service by teaching them that failure is but an inseparable part of life and getting back on track after falling, rather than avoiding it all together, is where true learning lies.

We are taught that the central portion of a Gaussian curve is where 95% of the population in any given sample lies. Well, that's what has been labeled 'normal;' and anyone beyond + 2 Standard Deviations (SD), an outlier. Naturally, it's much safer to be a part of the crowd, and if it works for you, pursue it by all means; but if it doesn't, respect your individuality enough to stop merely existing within these imaginary walls and start exploring beyond the 2SD restriction, that's when you start truly living. Would it be wise for all of us to walk the same path simply because it's validated by 'others' as 'conventional'? Growing out of the shackles of judgment and comparison was the most liberating feeling I have ever realized.

"Don't just aspire to make a living. Aspire to make a difference"

-Denzel Washington

I decided to institute an organization called A.S.P.I.R.E (Association for Support and Propagation of Innovation,

Research and Education); with the intent of supporting and nurturing the curiosity of this generation. Every single day, we all have brilliant ideas with the potential to revolutionize the world, but soon force ourselves into willfully ignoring them, because they are full of uncertainties. The idea of A.S.P.I.R.E for me was a similar intuition, a soft whisper at some corner of the mind, struggling to make itself heard in the loud noise and chaos of the external mediocrity, hell-bent on smothering it. My advice to all: ACT ON IT! Don't let the comfort of inaction drown out this little call of greatness from within. You never know what prospects it might have in store for you.

"You have to trust in something - your gut, destiny, life, karma, whatever. Because believing that the dots will connect down the road will give you the confidence to follow your heart even when it leads you off the well-worn path, and that will make all the difference."

Steve Jobs

And yes, in retrospect, the dots did connect. My ambitions did come with their own set of bureaucratic hurdles, nevertheless, after almost a year's grind; A.S.P.I.R.E. eventually became one of India's few student-led Medical Research and Innovation bodies. The gratification was not as much for establishing this organization per se, but the ability this gave me to believe in the strength of persistence, patience, and optimism. These experiences made me realize my love for administration and diplomacy, which eventually led me to quit the field of medicine post-M.B.B.S. and aim to become a Civil Servant, an Indian Foreign Service Officer. So, was it easy to make this decision? Of course not! And yes, I am afraid of stepping out into this new world; but I'll do it anyway, because, although I am afraid of fear, I am even more terrified of regret. So you do not need to be fearless, just don't let the fear overrun your desire to move past it.

When I envision my career, I choose to focus on the opportunity and not the obligation. I might fail and fall at some point in time, but my undergraduate days taught me to look into the eyes of the obstacle and get back up with a smile, only to continue the struggle. So, when asked, "Are you really going to change your career in spite of completing a lengthy and tough course like M.B.B.S?" I simply like to reply "I have finally realized my passion and the courage to pursue it only because of M.B.B.S"

Not having a vision for our lives is the greatest disservice we could do to ourselves. The only fish which go with the flow are the dead ones. Let every choice and decision of your life be an informed and conscious one. Unfortunate events and rough patches are bound to befall us, and more often than not, we won't have a say in these instances which break us. Nevertheless, our success lies in the ability to 'NEVER GIVE UP' and the choice between giving up and going; that is completely in our hands.

It's not easy, but it'll definitely be worth it.

Dr.Amanda Pereira

She did her MBBS from KJ Somaiya Medical College, Mumbai and her DNB General Medicine from Wanless Hospital, Miraj, Maharashtra. She is currently pursuing a fellowship in Diabetology at Wockhardt Hospital, Mumbai Central.

CHAPTER 12

A Patient's Journey - Through The Eyes Of A Doctor

Becoming a doctor teaches you a lot about medicine and people and life as well. But becoming a patient after being a doctor, makes you a better doctor and a better human too.

I was a second year Medicine resident at a tertiary care hospital in Miraj, Maharashtra, and was like any other average resident. My life revolved around attending rounds, calls, and emergencies, performing procedures, answering those weird queries of relatives that they were afraid to ask the consultants, spending sleepless nights, and having multiple cups of tea. I enjoyed it because I loved Medicine. I was learning something new each day, and I was getting the exposure I wanted.

Around 5 months after entering into my second year, I had a car accident a few kilometers away from the hospital where I worked. Because I immediately lost consciousness, I have no memory of what happened. All I remember is commotion, screaming, and a lot of pain - unbearable, excruciating pain.

"It was a major accident. You fell unconscious and had to be carried to the hospital. You dislocated your left hip, but along with that, there is a left acetabular fracture. Your acetabulum is reduced to pieces. We immediately did a closed reduction for the dislocation, but the fracture is complex and cannot be operated on here. You would have to go to either Mumbai or Pune. We have informed your parents

and some of your close friends. They are on their way," the Medical Superintendent of the hospital, an orthopedic surgeon himself, had told me after I had been stabilized.

The next day, I was shifted to Pune in an ambulance. I was operated on successfully at one of the best orthopedic institutes across the country. However, I required prolonged bed rest and physiotherapy. I was also informed about the possibility of developing post-traumatic arthritis in the future since the blood supply to the head of the femur had been compromised. If this happened, I might require a hip replacement. I was discharged after 14 days and was shifted to a lodging facility provided by the hospital for patients who wished to stay on for physiotherapy and further rehabilitation. My parents had shifted all our belongings into one room, where we would cook, sleep, and eat for the next six months.

I would put up my bravest face whenever the doctors came on rounds, or when my relatives and friends came to visit me. I would smile and joke and laugh like I am some superwoman with a fracture. The truth, however, was far from that.

I practically went through all the five stages of grief described by Kubler-Ross. Initially, I was in denial. I could not believe this had happened to me. It all felt like a horrible dream, and I was hoping to wake up from it. Then came anger and frustration. This was partly because of the severe pain I had which only subsided for a few hours with painkillers, but mostly because I was angry with God for letting this happen to me. *"Why me??"* was the only question that ran through my mind. Why did this have to happen now, when I was actually enjoying what I was doing? I should have been grateful I did not die, considering that the car involved in the accident had been damaged beyond recognition. Instead, I was angry about losing out on six months of residency training. Of all the things that could have worried me, I worried about whether I would be allowed to complete residency, and how I would complete my thesis. (Yes, can you imagine?)

Next came bargaining. I thought that maybe, if I exercised a little more, or if I didn't complain about the pain, I would recover faster. The pain did not let me sleep at night anyway, so I would play music at full volume on my headphones, and do whatever hand and leg exercises I was allowed while everyone snored away. I would practice spirometry so much that at one point I felt my lungs would burst. I Googled exercise videos and read articles about acetabulum fractures. I hid painkillers under my pillow and took 3 or 4 pills every night, apart from the ones I took in the day. All this continued until I developed severe gastritis, and passed out due to exhaustion and lack of sleep, and had my mother yell at me saying, *"YOU ARE A DOCTOR! WHAT DO YOU THINK YOU ARE DOING?"*

Then came the fourth stage - Depression. That was when the worst in me came out. I would cry. And cry. Then I would watch some TV. And cry a little more. Everything felt pointless. Although thinking like that feels foolish now, at that point in time, I thought this was it. This was the end of my life. Even if I recovered from this, I would still have some residual deformity. I would still have pain. I was doomed. On the nights where I did manage to sleep, I would wake up with nightmares.

When you have three months of absolute bed rest, and three months of minimal movement, it gives you a lot of time to think, probably much more than one would want. Our own thoughts terrify us more than anything else. But if we learn to listen to ourselves, the answers we seek lie right there - inside us. So, when I was done with all the crying and self-loathing and blaming life and blaming the inventors of cars, that is when I started to search for the meaning behind everything. Basically, I entered Stage 5 - Acceptance.

Sometimes, God throws a temporary pause in the middle of our life's journey. A pause that lets us reconsider things, and figure out where we are going wrong. That pause is not a waste. It is necessary because it shows us what truly matters, and what we should be pursuing. This was perhaps my pause. Or one of my pauses.

We all have this problem, where we let life get to us. We get so caught up in this race to do the best and be the best and have the best, that we often forget that our best does not only come from the work that we do. Our best also exists in the form of the bonds we nurture, and the time we spare for ourselves.

While it was true that I was in love with Medicine and all the new things that I was getting to learn, I had also pushed away every other thing that brought meaning into my life. Prayers, family, friends, relationships, sleep, health - everything had been neglected with this one excuse that I was 'doing residency' and I needed to 'focus on my career'. I avoided all phone calls from home, and never called back. I gave one-word replies to my friends when they needed me. And yet, they were all there for me, at one phone call. I had friends coming from Miraj and America and Dubai to visit me. I had relatives coming from near and far and patients who heard about my accident calling to check on me.

Although I lost out on a lot in those six months, what I gained was much more valuable. I gained perspective.

I learned how one person's illness can affect a family. I learned what mattered, and what did not. I learned compassion and forgiveness. I rediscovered the warmth of my mother's hugs and the wisdom in my father's lectures. I watched all the shows and movies I had missed out on. I read books. (No, not Harrison's textbook of Medicine. Novels.) My friend, who was doing his residency in Orthopedics at the institute where I was admitted, was with me throughout the surgery and through the entire phase of my recovery. Through him, I made some great friends and some even greater memories. Lying in one room for so long, I learned that with all its uncertainties and curveballs, life is still worth living.

During those six months of rehabilitation, I interacted with patients who had survived accidents much worse than mine. I met a 15-year-old who was paralyzed from the waist down, with a smile brighter than any I have ever seen. I met a 22-year-old who had lost both legs and his entire family in a tragic fire accident but was now a para-athlete. In all these people, I noticed one common thing. Their passion and zeal for life were much bigger than their setbacks. They let their pain fuel them, not stop them.

I also learned a few practical things. I learned the importance of frequent turning, and how to avoid bed sores. I learned that a Foley's catheter could hurt and that urination and defecation in the supine position is no easy task. It takes time to get used to it. I learned that even though an air mattress has air in it, it is still highly uncomfortable to sleep on. I learned that gastritis caused by NSAIDs is no joke, and constipation caused by opioids is no joke either. I learned that a spirometer is not just a toy, it actually makes a difference. I learned about disuse atrophy and contractures, and the absolute importance of constant Physiotherapy. I learned about how much we take our ability to walk and run and jump for granted. Most of all, I learned that in a doctor's life, a delay of 6 months or 1 year, or even 2 years means nothing. We are learners throughout our lives, and our opportunities to learn will never go away. I had kind and understanding professors, seniors, and colleagues, who supported and encouraged me through everything, even when I joined back.

I came to Pune with a fractured leg, pain, and remorse. But I left with a big smile, a heart filled with memories, the ability to walk on my own two feet again, and most of all, gratitude. Every patient that I have met since then, I have met with more respect and understanding. Because I had finally learned that we should never underestimate anyone's pain, whether physical or mental.

And sometimes, it is not medicine, but empathy, love, and kindness that can soothe pain.

Prakrut Paidisetty

Dr. Prakrut is an avid writer and medical researcher. He has published a rare medical case report and is currently working on 3 original research projects. He is a core team member at 'Lexicon- the medical magazine' and publishes frequently in the same. He has an intense desire to teach medical students and the general public alike. Therefore he participates in various NGOs to raise awareness about important public health issues! He loves to sing and is known for his humorous belly dancing skills!

CHAPTER 13

The Paradox

Of the many paradoxes in the life of a medical student, I want to highlight a paradox that each one of us thinks about at some point but never overthinks. What is it like for a medical student to get severely sick? For you young readers, I would like to make it clear, no doctor or medical student is immune to disease, and no matter how much we would like to think otherwise, it is a fact and backed by evidence. I would like to share one incident I faced in my First-year MBBS: here goes!

It was the monsoon of 2018; we were done with the theory papers of our university exams, nervously awaiting the practical exams and the vivas. I don't know if you ever faced this before, but there is this strange hunger that sets in two days before your vivas when you will be ready to eat absolutely anything. I also felt that hunger. In a series of bad decisions, I made a decision that I would go to the food stall outside my campus and eat what seemed like a dry plate of chicken noodles. Spoiler Alert: Monsoon and chicken noodles of food stallsdon't go hand in hand. So, there I was, after two hours, clenching my stomach, running a high fever, and thinking, "What have I done to deserve this?" Not to mention the constant bathroom visits, enough to have completed the entire quota of the boys' hostel that day. If you have learned basic biology you would know that excessive diarrhea causes severe dehydration, leading to a high fever and crippling body weakness, so much so that you cannot even walk straight! I was seriously in a poor state and thought to myself, like any other over-confident medical student, "I will get over this without any help!" That night was excruciating as every bite of food or every drop of water seemed to leave my body as soon as it entered. The next morning, I brought up the courage and told my roommate Yash about my plight. He gave me paracetamol to help me with my fever. Since I had not eaten or drunk anything, I did not have an episode of diarrhea after waking up, and the paracetamol helped with my fever. On the other hand, my best friend Neeti was getting frustrated because of my lack of response to her messages and absence from last night's dinner and today's breakfast. After I told her via text what happened, she requested me to come out and meet her at least once. I overestimated my recovery because I was still unable to walk normally; nevertheless, I went out to meet her, and she made me go to the hospital- her helping me along the longest five hundred meters of my life.

Truth be told, this was not my first case of indigestion in college, and as luck would have it, the intern who previously treated me for diarrhea was here again, and this time he was with his female colleagues who for some reason were flirting with me. The intern taunted me in Hindi and said, "Have you made a deal with diarrhea or what?". Ultimately due to my severe nature of the illness, I was directed to the medicine OPD- Neeti helping me go up and down the ramps and stairs like a true superhero. Now, the doctor was a very kind man who gave me a prescription for maybe an antibiotic and paracetamol. He suggested a liquid diet, and Neeti was kind enough to take me back to the outer gate of my hostel and bring some lentil-rice mashed for me to consume. As she could not enter the boys' hostel, she called Yash, who carried me the rest of the way. As soon as I took the first bite, the same story restarted, and I again went to the hospital, and this time the intern put me on IV saline and asked me what medications

I took. Contrary to popular belief, People do not become doctors as soon as they join MBBS, and it is natural for a first-year student to not be aware of what all drug names are and remember what he was prescribed. So, after this embarrassing incident, I took the saline, felt better, and went back to the hostel knowing fully well that I had to face an Anatomy viva the next day.

My fever hadn't come down, I was still weak, and the diarrhea condition had not improved. Relying on what I had studied in the past, I went to my Anatomy professors before the exam began and told them about my condition, to which they were surprisingly sympathetic. They also wrote me a prescription, and I was allowed to give my vivas first as opposed to my distally placed roll number. The vivas went surprisingly well, and then I headed back to my room before everyone else, worrying about the upcoming physiology practical the next day. They too were sympathetic to my plight and I was given first access to the grilling by the externals and HOD. Even after taking medication, my situation was not improving, and after the grueling session that was the biochemistry viva, I was free and had a decision to make. I had planned a trip with my school friends immediately after exams in Mumbai, but I chose to go home because life was just too nasty! I sat on a twelve- hour train ride to Agra, where I live, with no control over my luggage or my bowels. My parents, who learned about my condition, were worried and decided to pick me up at the station and were shocked to see me. What I did not mention to you readers was that I weighed 97 Kg when I first entered the med school, and at the end of my first year, I weighed 67 Kgs. After 30 kgs of weight loss, I recovered 30Kgs of humility and understood that no one is invincible! I finally recovered after completing the antibiotic course. The moral of my story is, we are not immune, but we cannot lose faith in the medical fraternity!

Dinesh Raja

Dinesh Raja is a philosophical human metamorphosing into the Doctor, presently in final year, Grant Medical College, Mumbai.

He is the Co-founder & Jt-Secretary of GMC Book club.

Currently a blogging intern in Lexicon, Online Medical Magazine and writes at WordPress under the name of, Ikiguy.

Born in Tirunelveli, partly raised in Pune, wholly in Mumbai, he is an ardent admirer of Bombay's sunsets.

A Medico by day, Musician by night,

He is a lover of Gardening, Peanut butter, and Bollywood.

He is a Curious otaku who's Passionately in love with Zindagi and believes what the world needs is, Love, True love.

CHAPTER 14

Sometimes A Cry Is All You Need

It was my first true outing in 8 and 1/2 months. Yippee, I was finally getting out of the locked-down home and rusted up grind.Alright, alright, I was just accompanying Amma for her office work in Bhusawal.Well, I know it may not be a big deal or vacation, but hey, this cruel corona has surely taught us all to appreciate and draw out bliss from the littlest of things. So, Bhusawal, the largest taluka in Jalgaon,The town of Bananas and White brinjal, *Vangi* as the Khandeshi people call it, here I come! It was an overnight train journey from L.T.T at midnight. For no particular reason, that evening, I was haunted by a question which was latent all these months and years, which used to surface occasionally, but when it did, it incapacitated me. Completely.

Did I make the right decision by becoming a doctor? That evening, just like the mid-life crisis, it felt as if I was going through a super - acute career crisis, and was questioning whether I made the right choice by getting into MBBS. I was looking back at my past self- when I had the chance to select, either the white coat or the various other passions which I could pursue.

Was it wise to spend so much time, energy, and youth to get into a medical college, and much more while surviving it?

Will I be happy slogging my entire life?

Will it be worth it at the end of our time?

Just when I needed some perpetual silence to comfort my incessant inner turmoil, there it was - My gift from the Beelzebub, the demon prince, tormentor of this night journey! I was blessed with the most obnoxious co-passenger ever, whose snoring was as rickety as Royal Enfield's silencer, whose sheer loudness would put Chernobyl's explosion to shame!

With some periorbital pain, I looked at my Mi Band, around 2 AM. With a lot of annoyance and irritation, I somehow managed to blow away those dark clouds, snuggled into a sleepy nimbus. *But again, does life work out the way we plan it?* Right, when the pain eased a bit, and my mind felt light-headed for the first time in hours, that's when I heard a night shattering scream that raged throughout the train compartment.

Commanding all the sleepy souls to wake up at once. It was a woman's scream. It felt full of pain and fear and helplessness. I genuinely felt that something really bad was happening to her. There were clicks of lamps turning on, murmurs of people, and shuffling of shoes. I woke up half irritated and half agitated, and was just wishing wholeheartedly that this was not a physical assault or even worse. I woke up sticky-eyed, feeling the fluids in my brain jiggling. As I was sitting cross-legged, I leaned forward a bit to locate the sound through the hallway. And instinctively I turned towards my right.

A saree clad woman, in her early 20s, collapsed near the train gate, screeching in pain. As my brain started to settle in, my eyes darted towards something creamy, a straw-colored globular thing that was protruding.As my ciliary muscles slowly accommodated that 6 feet distance, my pupils were taken aback. It was certainly a baby's head! Head of a new life, new birth, neonate!

Before I could even come up with the proper medical term for this, the head got delivered smooth as butter, and another scream filled the compartment. This one was different. It was chirpy, vibrant, and full of life. *There is definitely something very special when you hear a child's first cry. It simply transcends above every other sound you have heard in your entire lifetime.* At that moment, nothing else mattered.

My heart yearned to hear more of the outcry and feel the soft naiveness of the newborn. Luckily for both the mother and the baby, the labor happened at Kasara. Igatpuri station, which is a fairly big station, was a mere 20 minutes away. So, the T.T.E called up the station-in-charge and arranged for a gynecologist and an ambulance. While the mother was being tended to, I wrapped the infant in two secure sheets of cozy blankets. As I gave away the bundle of soft innocence to the doctor, I felt something.I felt as if the air around me expanded in warmth and flew away with the baby, taking my soul with it. For a moment it was. An unforgettable one. As I type down this story weary-eyed, on Google notes, my heart hums just one rhythm, Yes.Indeed. *It is worth it.*

P.S.: - The time when the baby boy took his first breath was 2.39 AM :)

I wish to sum up by penning down this poem below,

"The Path"

To blissfully romance, to play with biology, I chose this path.

To not indulge in physical gravity and chemical reactions, I chose this path.

To seek into the myriad depths of research, I chose this path.

To cherish my parents, smile with utmost satisfaction, I chose this path.

To see a lost friend smiling, that's what my heart wished for, I chose this path.

To see the poor souls relieved of incurable ailments, I chose this path.

To become the best healer, I chose this path.

And when thou ask me a thing or two to say,

on what made me trot in this unpredictable journey,

despite everything,

my modest spirit simply pours out...

Just when my insecure heart was wanting to race towards my home, friends became family, and obscure rooms became the happy hostel and made me stay.

Just when depression was choking away my soul, my playful idiots kicked the devil hard out of me and made me stay.

Just when perforating sadness penetrated ceaselessly through my heart, the soul, the smile over the lips of my patients, made me stay.

Just when the teary heart was ready to jump off because of battered bittered bonds; comfortable silence, releasing tears and a warm shoulder, made me stay.

Just when exhaustion was driving me to the brink, the cry of the naïve newborn made me get out of my slumber and made me stay.

Jairah Anna Jomilal

Jairah Anna Jomilal is a medical student at DY Patil medical college in Pune. An avid reader and writer , she has great passion for journalism and loves to engage in community work. She has been on a journey of self discovery and inner peace while in medical college and is excited to know what life has in store for her and determined to make the best of every opportunity in life.

CHAPTER 15

Is Curing Pain, Worth The Pain?

Most medical students, when asked why they chose the profession, would answer one of two things- they want to contribute to society by saving lives, or they want the respect and social standing that doctors so generously receive. Armed with a white coat and a bag full of books, they enter medical college with a lot of dreams, hopes, and expectations. But no amount of tv shows or movies could ever prepare a fresher for the medicos experience. It's not to say they weren't warned by seniors about how stressful the exams and schedules would be, not to mention the never-ending coursework. Despite the warning, most enter into a mental/ emotional breakdown within the first two years. The lucky ones stick it out till the end of their degree, only to be frustrated later on in their careers. Add to all this the callous attitude to violence against doctors and the general insensitivity to their issues, and one can't help but wonder, Is it truly worth it all? Doctors sacrifice their youth, their sleep, their hobbies, and their personal life to earn their degree, all through it telling themselves that this is what they have to do to help save lives, to make a difference, but the increasing number of attacks against doctors seem to prove otherwise. So, what then will inspire future generations of medicos to take up the profession?

Life as a doctor is tough and unrelenting. The medical college and the highly competitive environment in which it operates are supposed to prepare the students to succeed in a highly demanding career. Despite this, there is an increase in the number of attempted suicides by students, some of them even postgraduate students. Most medical colleges report one or two suicides every year. According to WebMD, a doctor commits suicide every day in the USA, a figure higher than the military-which is considered to be a more stressful profession. Around the world, the suicide rates for doctors are higher than the general population. Figures from World Health Statistics show that in India, there are 16.3 suicides for every one lakh of the population, whereas for the rest of the world the figure is 10.6. This means that in a country with an all too high number of suicides, suicides among doctors and medical students are something of a public health crisis, given the alarming frequency with which it happens. In a country where doctors are expected to be God, a doctor, or a medical student with mental health issues would be severely stigmatized and suffer career-wise. The Covid 19 pandemic has, to some extent, shed a light on the plight of healthcare workers, and cases of doctor or student suicides, violence against doctors, and underpaid or exploited healthcare workers, which were underreported before, are now being diligently reported by the media. Unfortunately, the pandemic has also aggravated the problem by increasing the stress and workload of hospital staff that was already overworked.

As stated before, the current situation of doctors and medical students is something of a public health crisis, which needs quick action to mitigate the problem before it further complicates an overwhelmed system. Perhaps the first step to be taken is recognition by the government and various associations that this is a crisis that needs swift handling. Stringent measures against those who attack or otherwise harass or abuse medical professionals, holding hospitals and medical colleges to greater accountability for the work environment they provide, and greater awareness among the general public that this is a problem that needs to be addressed is key to slowing down the current upward trend of suicide and workplace dissatisfaction. An exam pattern that is more student-friendly, supportive professors and teaching staff in medical colleges can go a long way in improving not only the mental health of students but also enhance the productivity and the standard of learning as well. One of the best ways to help those suffering from depression would be through support groups and NGOs dedicated exclusively to the mental health of healthcare workers.

As the pandemic has shown, healthcare workers are essential service workers. Without development in medical science, our world today would have been a very different place. Indeed, to them, we owe our lives, as they so bravely risk their health and much more for the benefit of humanity. And it is high time that we remove the pedestal we put them on, recognize their needs, and support a very misunderstood yet crucial section of our society.

Mahin Bhatt

Mahin Bhatt is a final year medical student in Mumbai with a keen interest in research, medical education, writing and a wide variety of extracurricular activities in addition to pursuing academic and clinical excellence.

He secured the first rank in his college in the I MBBS university examinations and has won several panel discussions and quizzes at prestigious conferences.

He was awarded the ICMR - Short Term Studentship in 2017.

He was one of the Tata Scholars for 2019-20 and was awarded a scholarship in Oncology to Tata Memorial Hospital, Mumbai and Guy's Hospital, King's College London.

He is on the editorial committees of student run magazines and is also actively interested in providing medical services to the marginalized. He has volunteered extensively with several organizations and has managed the Medical Education and Health Awareness projects of student-run NGOs.

CHAPTER 16

Learning Beyond The Classroom

Nobody and nothing can prepare you for medical college. Contrary to popular belief, it doesn't matter if your parents are doctors or how stellar your academic record has been, or how many seminars you have attended before starting your medical journey. The first few days of medical school are a uniformly disorienting experience. Partly because of the grueling six months of entrance exams, merit lists, cut-offs, paperwork, and a cantankerous clerk-laden admissions process or the two harrowing years of exam preparation that precede it.

But mainly, because one goes from being a school or a college student to someone who, over the next half-decade will learn not only the intricacies of the human body but also the art of caring for people at their most vulnerable, the ability to make decisions under unfathomable pressure and be skilled enough to hold another's life in one's own hands. And so, one enters the hallowed lecture theaters and laboratories of medical college with a queer mix of fear, excitement and without the faintest idea of the responsibilities, moments of joy, self-doubt, successes and setbacks, tears and smiles that lie in store.

Gone are the days of spoon-feeding and hand-holding. Now, the first few lectures start with the briefest of orientations before diving into the syllabus. It's like learning to swim by jumping into the deep end of the pool.

With the advantage of hindsight, I can now attest to the fact that most people who join MBBS are painfully unaware of what this course entails or the subjects one will have to study, and much to the amusement of seniors and teachers, some newly admitted students even struggle with the full name of the course. None of these lacunae reflect poorly on their potential or enthusiasm but are simply a representation of our socio-cultural milieu that encourages students with a vague liking for biology and school-level science to become doctors. Luckily for everyone involved, most incoming medical students are the brightest minds of their generation, with an abiding sense of duty to the society they inhabit and a deep affection for the life sciences.

My own journey started in 2016 after a particularly confusing entrance exam season and admissions process. Luckily, I'd secured a government college seat. It just happened to be four hundred kilometers away from home. I should have been counting my blessings that it was still in my state, that I spoke the state language, that I could travel comfortably by rail or road, and most importantly that it was a well-known institution, but to my eighteen-year-old mind, leaving the comfort of home and the cosmopolitan familiarity of Mumbai was just positively depressing.

It dawned upon me, not long after starting college, that this was the most formative, life-changing time and an experience that I now proudly refer to as 'the best thing that has ever happened to me'. Living away from home or joining MBBS are independently major positive disruptions, but together they alter one's approach to life. The most important factor was undoubtedly the people I met, all of whom had something to teach me, unique experiences unlike any of mine that taught me the value of examining situations from all perspectives.

One of my biggest learnings came during my application for an ICMR Short Term Studentship, an undergraduate research grant. I was applying in my first year, which already ruffled many feathers, and to make things worse, the topic I had chosen was completely clinical. After weeks of missed lunches, protocol formulating, and meeting unnecessarily exacting requirements, I had submitted a relatively fool-proof protocol to the ethics committee for review.

And so, I strolled in on the day of the meeting expecting a small, civilized question and answer session with a few well-meaning suggestions. It was, to put it mildly, a massacre. The committee members were reading the protocols for the first time during the meeting and had come only to fixate on some irrelevant detail and butcher the applications and the applicant's egos. Everyone around me remained unfazed by this institutional hazing but being the youngest of the lot, I took it all rather personally.

Of course, my project was approved and I was even awarded the ICMR stipend but I learned one central truth of medicine, that however much you know, there's more to learn and that you will never be truly, completely prepared for every situation.

As time passed, I secured academic and extracurricular prizes and experiences that facilitated encounters with eminent doctors, the movers, and shakers of their disciplines, and brilliant students who broadened my horizons. But the most impactful moments were also the least conspicuous, the ones that happened in the quiet corners of wards. When I learned to look beyond the exciting cases, unique findings, and see the people, their stories, fears, and faith. The most valuable education any medical student can receive is that we are in this to treat patients as a whole and not just their diagnoses.

Nowhere was this drilled into me more than during my visits to Tata Memorial Hospital. I had volunteered at TMH in my second year to help patients and their relatives navigate the crowds and queues. In my third year, I attended the prestigious Foundations in Oncology program and was subsequently awarded a scholarship to visit both Tata Memorial Hospital and Guy's Hospital, London as an observer to gain valuable insights into the varied field of oncology, which sees people at their most vulnerable, who despite their illnesses possess an innate, unshakeable strength.

As I write this essay, I am reminded that our biggest teachers are the patients who tell us infinitely more than books ever can, if only we were to stop and listen, and remind us that we often forget to see them as more than their diagnoses.

Many people sail through these five and a half formative years without much to show, but it's a period of relative freedom, with all the privileges that youth brings, sans any major responsibilities, with a universe of resources at our fingertips, leaving us limited only by the extent of our ambition. MBBS is truly what you make of it.

Pooja Suchday

First doctor to be in a family hierarchy of lawyers. Medicine for her, happened rather out of the blue; what drove her towards it was her inquisitiveness about the omnipresent why's and how's of human functionality.

She is currently volunteering with a number of governmental public awareness, and teaching programmes focussed on female and child health and intends to continue playing her part in the larger goal of improving public health at its core.

Articulate and opinionated, she has excelled in many public debates and extempores.

An avid reader, prefers books to humans anyday; her words often find salvation in penned down poems.

When not worked up, she can be found strumming her guitar; sketching; or hiking up a mountain, beholding backdrops.

Believes that "*The mind has colossal capabilities, and we only sail seas we're meant to dive in*"

She remains a seeker.

CHAPTER 17

A Student Of Life

"I would become anything but a doctor" I used to say. And here I am, transmuted, writing about how I ended up in the third year of medical school; the ebb and flow of my time in it.

"Any college but this" I would say, only to land up in the very same college, having found a bunch of people who I know will have my back for life, and I am ever grateful.

Life has always come back to me saying, "I am not the picture you have painted in your mind of me, it is your artistry; I have surprises to offer, you have to let down the contrivances in order to conjure the unmanifest".

Three years have been quite a journey, changing my entire outlook towards life. *Verily, I was ever blooming.*

With a history of straight distinctions throughout school, my approach to studying was meticulous, covering the entire book. (You can laugh because this becomes impossible in MBBS, where your retention eventually gives way, a fact I was unaware of back then.) It was a time-consuming method—touching on every part but mastering none. Those so-called "important questions" seemed like a sham to me (although, believe me, they are lifesavers on the final day).

During my first year University exams, my roommate fell sick and moved to a relative's place after the first one. So, I had been living alone during the rest of them. It was cataclysmic.

At that time, I had mental snowstorms like never before. The cauldron of anxiety from trying to revise an entire year's content in one night; the inability to rationalize; barely living on a four hour sleep schedule and not eating straight up for twenty-four hours because there just wasn't enough time. My circadian rhythm was messed up to a point where I just didn't have enough energy at the end of a three hour exam.

I passed with fairly good grades, albeit in a devastating state of mind.

I knew I had it all wrong.

Back then, grades were sacrosanct for me. During the beginning of my second year, I had decided to stop the exam-oriented approach. By that I mean, I decided to delve deeper into the enigma of subjects, trying to understand more and developing a holistic approach, going back and forth the books of first and final year alongside, to have a complete gist of whatever new I was exploring.

This was about the time when I actually started enjoying the learning process, rather than doing it out of compulsion.

That year, I achieved distinction with a university and college rank. Surprisingly, it no longer provided satisfaction. I began to realize that the vastness of this field was beyond full comprehension. Being a doctor isn't the culmination of knowledge but a continual journey. Whether in the first year or after a decade of practice, it's an ongoing exploration, striving for precision in a challenging profession, where there's no guarantee of cure, but we persist.

During this period, I delved into new genres, particularly psychiatry, philosophy, and folklore. Medical school is challenging, and students often sacrifice their mental well-being. I sought my own space to nurture a healthy mind.

Then came 2020, a year etched in everyone's memory. The pandemic began to spread, disrupting the world.

Being in my space for long periods permitted me a lot of self-exploration. I did online clinical courses offered by international universities; read more effectively; about Ayurveda, yoga, nutrition, anything that would as little as fascinate me. It helped me realize that as intricate, complex, and diverse diseases are (which, we acquire extrinsically) so is the human inability to maintain what is intrinsically his- A HEALTHY LIFESTYLE.

I practically visited the hospital daily, being closely posted about a case; I lost someone I deeply loved and respected.

I learned.

So, anyone reading this, having a hard time going through one more day of the tediously long hours of reading, hoping for their misery to end, times to change, know that they will not, not the way you would want them to, but your vantage of it can. Once you start enjoying the process, your subconscious will stop asking for an escape.

Now, more than ever, I continue to seek knowledge, not only from books and collaboration with brilliant minds but also from life's diverse experiences, whether related to medicine or not.

The knowledge that we gain is well borrowed and steered in Perpetuum, but our experiences whilst going about it are magnetic. That alone, my friend, commensurates *raison d'être.*

Yours truly,

A student of life.

P. Charulata Sree

She is P. Charulata Sree, a goal oriented dental student by day and a reader by night.

She has always loved a good read and this quarantine gave her a chance to take it a step further by channeling her thoughts and experiences in a book.

She feels a smile is the most natural yet the most powerful gift and is obliged to give someone that confidence and happiness. She is ambitious and driven and loves a new challenge every now and then. Being a research enthusiast, she is currently hustling between different methodologies while working on her own research. Currently she's the state ambassador of 'Dentowesome', a community of dental students from all over the country and a frequent writer on their blog as well. She is compassionate and empathetic in nature who certainly wishes to make the world a better place.

CHAPTER 18

Dental School Diaries

Freshly graduated from school, I had no ideas or opinions on oral healthcare. Maybe because a majority of Indians still don't consider dentists as the 'real' doctors, I never really gave a thought to becoming one. But as I toiled hard for months to crack the pre-medical examination and found my peace with physics, chemistry, and biology, the situation that caught my eye was how oral health in our country was taken for granted. I came across people suffering from unbearable pain but still refusing to go to a dentist for the needful. The Indian *jugaad* is what they would prefer rather than a professional treatment! This absurd mindset shifted my focus to oral healthcare.

A new city, new milieu; as I stepped into dental school, I realized I didn't even know what kinds of dental specialties there were, how different this journey will be compared to MBBS or how the process of dental school itself even worked. But I had this weird, undeniably strong, intuitive feeling that this is what I was meant to do...and all I knew was that I had to follow it.

I truly feel that a smile is the most natural yet the most powerful gift we possess as humans. It's magical, it's striking, it's courageous. It's the physical expression of love, gratitude, kindness, happiness, excitement, content, understanding, and pleasure. It's a universal language! Even when a language barrier can stop clear communication, a genuine smile can show your kindness. Imagine if you couldn't smile, laugh, comfortably eat or drink, or express your emotion. Whether you were embarrassed or if you had a condition that caused you pain, if you were born with a deformity that had been ridiculed, or looked at yourself in the mirror and felt your smile wasn't pretty enough. This, to me, is misery. While there were students in my class who were sorrowful about missing out on an MBBS seat, all I could think of was how beautiful dentistry is. A perfect blend of art and science, working to beautify things as well as restoring their function! This and my compassion and empathy for people fused with the unique balance of holistic care are some of the reasons why I thought dentistry was my calling.

The first year in college was exciting, from being in awe of the different branches this field offered to the zing of making new friends, I was ready to step into this world. Dental anatomy and histology were my first peek at this new universe. Carver was used more like a toy than an instrument at first. There were wax shavings all over the desk, floor, bag, and even my apron. *Oh, how I loved the slippery feel of the room!* Slowly I learned to shape the wax block dexterously and artistically as a tooth. From RFT's to urine analysis, biochemistry gave me a nostalgic ride down the school lane. Physiology is where we pricked fingers and wore stethoscopes for the first time; for the naïve me that was my first glimpse into the medical world. But the most thrilling experience was dissecting the cadaver in the anatomy lab. Even though the smell of formaldehyde was nauseating, it couldn't stop us from posing for pictures with organs! Second year was all about the preclinical experience. The agony of teeth arrangement in prosthodontics, especially while using a Bunsen burner in summers! Conservative lab was all about the precision required to make the cavity walls smooth in a typodont and mastering the art and attention to detail rather than the speed of the procedure. From juggling between slides in microbiology and pathology to the tongue-twisting drugs in pharmacology, studies became more serious and I could feel the intricacy level increasing. And just like that, the second year was over in a jiffy. But now as a third year student with hindsight, I realize that each day brings a new set of challenges. Working on patients rather than phantom heads has been the most difficult yet rewarding aspect of the course to me. Though there were days when I missed how the phantom heads did not fog up my mirror nor did they have a rebellious tongue ready to push my instruments away making me readjust my finger every 10 seconds, and certainly never had an anxiety or panic attack on the dental chair! But the satisfaction of interacting with a patient, acknowledging their pain and dilemma, and getting to know them on a personal level, does outweigh these minor drawbacks.

Practicing in a small town surrounded by working-class people, I realized how people still fear the dental surgeon. Patients are rather paternalistic and leave all the decisions to the dentist. Despite the availability of dentists in rural areas, the barriers that limit access to dental care were lack of awareness, transportation issues, and the ability to pay. These issues are making it difficult for them to acknowledge the importance of regular dental visits. Once I came across a woman in her late 50's with minor pain in one of her posterior teeth. Inspecting further, I found a thick white patch on her oral mucosa. On palpating, the lesion appeared non-scrapable. Keeping in mind her tobacco consumption, it was then diagnosed as leukoplakia, an often- misdiagnosed premalignant lesion. I wondered how a simple dental visit saved her from the agony of suffering from a malignant disease.

I have had patients who come in saying they 'hate dentists' and further conversation with them reveals that they actually hated 'stems' from a bad experience. I want to make sure that everyone I treat has a positive encounter and a surge in confidence concerning professional treatment. The happiness of a successful root canal treatment, a simple restoration to subside pain, or even a denture to enjoy foods they may have previously struggled with, can come immediately on completion of treatment when you look at the satisfaction on the patient's face. But sometimes, it's a short-lived sensation as treatments can take weeks or months of hard work. So that's why I have decided to enjoy my journey rather than the destination; I hope you enjoy yours.

Elizabeth Shama Rini

M. Elizabeth Shama Rini, born and raised in the city of Hyderabad is a House surgeon who is the first in her family to take up this profession. Growing up, she was always fascinated by Medicine and loved to play doctor with her friends. Now, Years later, she is close to obtaining the degree of her dreams. She is a high achiever academically and creative at the core, frequently dabbling in music, art and writing. Ambitious, Inquisitive, Proactive – are the three words that describe her best.

When she's not binge-watching true crime documentaries or superhero movies, you'll find her in her room jamming to 165 different genres of music. She aims to increase conversation about mental health and stigma surrounding various topics. She desires to give back to the community in full measure.

CHAPTER 19

An Open letter to Medical Students

Hello stranger,

I hope this letter finds you in good spirits. Having trudged a great way through the wild waters of Medical School, I believe I am capable of proffering some advice so you can take the bitter with the sweet. *No, these are not study tips.*

No matter where you've pitched your tent currently – either at the starting point with your NEET UG or at the boss level with your NEET PG or anywhere in between, this is for you.

The road you've chosen is long, tortuous and labyrinthine. It will make you wish you had taken up math instead of science when you had the chance. It might make every other course seem easier but you can bet your bottom dollar that it is gratifying.

The time you spend in Med-school will be the fastest 4½ years of your life. You will go from dissecting a cadaver to diagnosing a case in the blink of an eye.

My first advice to you is – **Set that alarm!** In fact, set multiple! Do you know that little voice in your head that convinces you that you can wake up early despite staying up all night? It's lying to you.

You don't want to be the last one to enter your class and get the looks only a criminal would get. You don't want to make a crazed run from your mess to the early dissection class that my friends and I are familiar with. Because halfway through, you will realize you forgot your apron and have to run back. Even if you do make it, you'll end up thirsty because you forgot your water bottle somewhere. *Drat!*
On a serious note, Punctuality is as important as excellence or altruism in our profession. You don't want to run late during emergencies, Do you?

Second, **don't let stress consume you.** There will be subjects you love and ace. They will be subjects you love but suck at. There will be subjects you absolutely hate. *PSM, I'm looking at you.* You will certainly have too much on your plate. Still, I must urge you to not lose yourself in this hustle and bustle.

Let's be real. This is not a movie in which the protagonist can drop everything and go find themselves in the Himalayas. *I doubt there's more reality on the top of Mount Everest than there is in the park close by. But, that's a story for another day.*

Make as many mistakes as you can because this is the only place where it is allowed. Learn from them and you won't repeat them in the future.

Pace yourself. Set realistic goals. Don't compare yourself to others. Remember what Theodore Roosevelt said – Comparison is the thief of joy.
Above all, Strive to the best of your efforts.

Third, **Cultivate tolerance.** Leave your prejudices at the door.

It is said that the best physicians do not judge. Losing your objectivity can lead to improper medical care. Age, Sex, Gender, Caste, Religion, Creed or social status shouldn't faze you. *If you ask me, nothing you list in the case sheet should make you think twice.* Don't be stingy with your compassion.

Our profession is one of the few that requires complete obliteration of preconceptions. It is one that requires us to view a human being as just that - a human being. *Can you imagine a world like that?*

Four, **Make the most of your breaks.** Holidays are the best thing since sliced bread for any college student. *No kidding!*

It is important that we learn to consistently and completely disconnect from laborious schedules. Studying Medicine can suck energy straight from our souls. Learn an instrument or two. Reclaim yourself through your pastimes. Improve yourself in areas that you find are lacking. Take a walk with your dog or do gardening with your mom. *Do whatever but don't carry this stress home!*

Finally, **Check in on yourself and your friends frequently.** Anxiety, Depression and Mental breakdowns are on the rise owing to the learning and assessment methods in universities. The least we can do is regularly and actively connect to manage our triggers and combat burnout. *Remember to never hesitate to ask for help.*

It is only after you enter Medical school that you realize it is obviously different from our pretend games. Doctors don't just fly in and save the day. A good physician requires years of training, love for science, a modicum of intelligence and sheer willpower.

Excellence, Altruism, Humanism and accountability are words that frequently resonate within the walls of every medical school. These are the virtues every aspiring doctor must master.

Pursuing Medicine has both pros and cons. You might've been attracted to the fact that doctors save lives. But here, you will also witness a doctor deliver bad news to someone. You will witness a colleague suffer from impostor syndrome. You'll have to face trials and tribulations during your unending schooling. And when you receive heartfelt gratitude from a patient, you will have found your reason to keep going.

As the years pass, you'll learn to align your goals and values. This profession will give you a platform to voice your message. *Make sure it's a good one!*

When you are awarded your degree, it doesn't magically make you a skilled physician. The white coat doesn't make you a professional. The change is insidious, catalyzed by failures and successes alike.

When you leave Medical school, you leave with a gift that keeps on giving. You leave with the knowledge that the weight of the stethoscope symbolizes the responsibility you shoulder – of a person's life, a family's future and society's change. Your apron will be a reminder of your commitment to do no harm.

So, take these years to truly learn and love. Soon, you'll be able to change the world, one patient at a time.

Wishing you the best on your journey,

Yours truly.

Parvathy Mohanan

Parvathy Mohanan is a medical student from Medical University Sofia, Bulgaria. She is an avid researcher and has been a part of numerous publications. She has also participated and organized many international medical conferences. She also runs a leisure society promoting debate and healthy discussions on relevant topics from different genres. She has volunteered for medical camps associated with the Red Cross. She strongly endorses demonetization of fundamental healthcare and everyone's right to attain quality healthcare regardless of their social and economical status.

Incessant Legacy

Dr. Mary Walker, Dr. Mary Ponnen Lukose, Dr. Dorothy Lavinia Brown Dr. Mirudhubashini Govindarajan, Dr. Chithrthara Gangadharan, Karimpat Mathangi Ramakrishnan - few names from the long list of doctors and their chronicles that inspired me to take up this path. I believe that I'm in a time and era that is far better than it was for these ladies and getting refined day by day, painfully slow but metamorphosing. I was living in a bubble where I thought gender discrimination is a pathogen that the medical field is immune to, at least in western countries. A world where your intelligence and skills spoke stronger than the threshold you fall on the gender spectrum. Alas, a hospital is also a workspace that has all the flaws of any other workspace, donned by male supremacy on the pillars of patriarchy.

"The higher you go the fewer women there are"

- Chimamanda Ngozi Adichie

During my winter break, my roommate, a fellow medical student, and I began our internship in the Department of Gastroenterology in a military hospital. We were in the 3rd year at the time with half a semester of internal medicine done up to cardiology, but the plight was that we hadn't yet studied gastroenterology as it would be part of the syllabus in the second semester. On our first day, we were agonizing over the audacity we had to walk into a gastroenterology ward without even knowing the cardinal difference between Crohn's disease and ulcerative colitis. We have all heard gore stories of petrifying doctors or specialist registrars who would stamp you down to rock bottom, beyond your self-esteem and we were prepared to face that debacle. A roller coaster ride indeed, a concoction of excitement, incompetence, and surrealness with which we walked into the ward. The head of the department, our designated doctor, and the nurses were extremely warm and solicitous, much to our surprise. They guided us through countless endoscopies, colonoscopies, and endoscopic retrograde cholangiopancreatography. The anaesthesiologist instructed us on how to perform an intramuscular injection with saline solution on a sedated patient whose consent was obviously taken before the procedure, at least I think he did. Every morning before the rotations all the doctors met up in a common room for coffee and morning banter and we hung around them assuming that we are as cool as them.

One morning, the anaesthesiologist- who was a very warm and nice person- asked me what specialty I wanted to go for and I said orthopedic surgery. He gasped and I quote "why would a beautiful girl like you go into orthopedics?.. It's a carpenter's job! And surgery?" Nodding his head in disapproval. He wrapped his abysmal sexist virtue around a sugar-coated compliment leaving me puzzled on how to react. The cherry on top was our assigned doctor complaining about how the gastroenterology association elected the first woman as their president in 30 years, just because she is a woman! Not because she's talented and deserving but she won the elections just because she is a woman. A second ago I was told orthopedics or surgery as a whole is not my cup of tea, because I'm a girl and then someone comes along and says people achieve higher designations just because they are a woman. So, are they blind that they don't see gender discrimination? It's understood that it is the result of their conditioning of years old patriarchy leading them to believe these false abstract conclusions but I expected doctors to be more unprejudiced. As doctors, it should be absolutely clear that we human beings are not just a bag of muscles but an amalgamation of cerebral power, physical strength, and endurance.

The centuries-old method of using basic biology as the optimum will leave us stagnant as a whole nation. Of course, there's a claim that things are changing now, in fact, statistically proven - The Canadian Institute for Health Information (CIHI) report shows that now the overall ratio of doctors is different from 50 years ago where the average of female doctors grew up to 42 percent in 2018 from 11 percent in 1978. It is also true that more than 10% of female physicians have experienced workplace sexual assault compared to just 4% of men. 50 % of women who have experienced sexual assault and harassment stated that this harmed their career, rendering to a Medscape survey. The harassment often provides exposure to sexist jokes or a lower income. The wage gap is yet another grievous reality that is still non-perishable in this world. A study conducted in 1990 showed that the mean earnings of male doctors were $155,400, while the female doctors were making mean earnings of $109,900, with a difference of $45,500, less than compared to their contemporary male doctors. We no longer use electric gadgets from the 90s but somehow this phenomenon is running smoothly as shown in the NHS in the UK currently with a 17% gender pay gap which means that the average hourly earnings of all female employees are 17% less than the average hourly earnings of all male employees.

All this data proves that it is excruciatingly slow, but circumstances are evolving with time for the enhancement of gender equality, simultaneously portraying ample enough room for improvement. The change is substantially inspiring to young girls and boys aspiring to become doctors in a society that values gender equality. Henceforth, we have to work together to further widen the path that once used to be a dark hole. Thousands of women before us set pivotal examples so that the future generation can have it in its prime. Whenever someone tells you that you can't be a successful surgeon just because you are a woman, you always have a T. S Kanaka to button their lip. So, don't be disheartened by the persisting discrimination or settle down when you see the syrupy statement "things are changing". You have to make history to change it and to do so, you have to set an example that will be a testimonial to the future generation. Just remember that the glass ceilings are shattered already, and now the sky is your limit.

Gayathri Menon

Gayathri is an ambitious young doctor who just finished her M.B.B.S from Yenepoya Medical College, Mangalore. Raised in Dubai and having completed her high school from one of the top boarding schools in India at Chinmaya International Residential School- Coimbatore, she is fortunate to have grown up in a culturally diverse background. Apart from maintaining an excellent academic profile throughout her medical school, she has been a part of numerous healthcare projects at a community level. She also has a keen interest in reading, writing and is an active member with honorable positions in numerous student-run medical organizations of national and international recognition.

Being a Gen-Z doctor with a primary interest in Internal Medicine, she is also quite passionate about space and hopes to be able to learn more about Travel and Space Medicine in the future. As an ardent follower and preacher of Bioethics, she firmly believes that all treatment must be in the best interest of each patient and hence aspires to lead by example.

CHAPTER 21

The Uncooperative Patient

"To study the phenomenon of disease without books is to sail an uncharted sea, while to study books without patients is not to go to the sea at all." One of my professors said this to me in our very first class by quoting the great physician Sir William Osler. A doctor will have to come across many patients every day. This also means that each patient is given equal time and respect. After all, no disease or illness can be learned better without seeing the patient.

Having spent almost 4 years in a medical college, I have experienced all sorts of things. Many of them are worth mentioning. Some anecdotes have left footprints in my heart that I wish I could explain. However, if there is anything that I have always wanted to write about in my field, it would be this. Hereby, I would like to talk about "the uncooperative patient".

Many times, we have used the common sentence "The patient was uncooperative". In fact, this sentence has been misused so much by medical students that one often uses it as an excuse to skip the examination. It is not correct of me to state facts like this without accepting that I too have done the same at some point in my yesteryears. But how frequently are we casually throwing in this excuse?

While it is common to see students misuse this phrase it is seldom that one comes across a teacher who does so. This is one such incident that I vividly recollect.

It was a surgery class, and we were asked to take the case of a lump in the breast. The breast is a private organ and isn't something that we get to see many times before the exam. So when we were assigned this case, we were obviously interested. The patient, a middle-aged woman in her late forties, was very gentle and kind. She answered our numerous questions and did not mind us repeatedly interrogating her about the lump. Now, since this was a case that would be kept for our exams, there were about twelve of us who wanted to examine her. I do not know if there is a cutoff to say at what point patients can be labeled uncooperative. But I do know this- the breast isn't something a lot of women would be comfortable exposing. Nevertheless, our patient proved surprisingly calm. She permitted us to examine her lump and we all took turns to understand what it could be. This might sound alarming to many people. But occasionally, some patients do allow us, medical students, to examine them in such large numbers. She was one such patient. I was one of the first among us to examine her breast. So while the others were examining it after me, I couldn't help but imagine the plight of the patient. I tried placing myself in her shoes for a few moments and immediately shuddered. The idea of having multiple people touch my breasts, despite them being budding doctors seemed mortifying. At this point, I must mention that although we were many people, our sole intention was only to study and understand her condition to sharpen our clinical skills.

Soon we were done examining and had to bring her to the classroom where the case presentation and discussion would happen. The professor in charge of teaching us entered the room and a wave of authoritativeness washed upon us. A friend of mine presented the case and when the examination part was being discussed, the sir wanted to demonstrate it to us to ensure that we learned the correct method.

Despite being a final year medical student, I cannot even imagine what it must feel like to be the subject of examination and looked upon as a specimen. Of course, medically speaking, I have moved past the phase of seeing body parts that are not conventionally exposed. But from a patient's perspective, it is out of routine to expose yourself for two hours and be viewed through the eyes of scrutiny. Consent is something that plays a huge role in such situations. So, after obtaining informed consent, the doctor in charge began to show us the various methods of palpation and what to look for, all while our patient exposed herself to us.

This went on for about an hour or so and the professor, having completed the whole examination, was concluding. But a breast examination is never complete without examining the lymph nodes in the armpit. Hence, after completely palpating her breasts and making her go through this uncomfortable procedure for those two hours, he moved on to palpate the lymph nodes. At this point, our patient was fed up and wanted to leave. This was indeed a very understandable reaction from a woman of her age who had been exposed and examined for so long. As a result, she did not consent to her lymph node examination and the sir let her go saying, "she is uncooperative".

Now being a doctor with certain years of experience, it is common to see all kinds of patients. And while it is wrong to categorize them, it is true that in their medical odysseys, they might have encountered some patients who were slightly more cooperative than the others. But having said that, each patient is different, and it is impossible to compare them with respect to their conditions and how each one handles them.

It enraged me to see that although our patient cooperated so well and was so compliant with the whole procedure, the doctor called her "uncooperative". I was completely taken aback when he let her go with a subtle 'thankyou' that merely escaped from his mouth.

Patients can indeed be uncooperative at times, particularly when so many students pester them to complete their case sheet writing on the same day. But while all this is part of the many cons that go with getting admitted to a teaching hospital, it is important to not lose sight of the fact that patients are humans too. A little kindness can go a long way and it is pertinent to be sensitive to the emotional turbulence that we medical students cause them at times.

Ananya Vadhera

Ananya Vadhera is pursuing MBBS from Maulana Azad Medical College (2018). She has always been fascinated by the marvels of the human body. As a research enthusiast, she has published papers on migraine related disability and pediatric nephrology. She takes pride in being a good communicator and showing compassion towards her patients. Born in India, brought up as a child in the USA and UK, she has interacted with people from various cultures. She has been a part of many medical organizations where she tries to make a positive impact on public health and professional development. From being a graceful Bharatanatyam dancer, a skillful debater, and an avid reader to winning laurels in basketball, badminton and marathons, she walks the walk of personal mastery. She strongly believes that no one should have to die when they can be saved, and one day, she hopes to save many lives.

CHAPTER 22

Stepping Stones

Proud, teary eyes looking down at me. Hug, kisses and smiles all around.

"I'm so proud of you." The words that make all efforts pay off.

My journey on this road began with a lot of joy. After two years of juggling between engineering and medical coaching, I made it to one of the most reputable colleges in the country, and with a rank that I could only dream of. Here began my life of newer and richer experiences.

From my dissection hall diaries where I witnessed the anatomy of the human body in its glorious entirety and the feel of cutting ribs below my hands to being guided by seniors for our postings, medical school has a lot to offer.

During my first and second year, I had the opportunity to visit and lead a health camp. It reminded me of the privilege I have with access to information and good healthcare. The leadership experience, the networking opportunity of talking to organizers who were well past their 60s and had been making such a huge difference in the lives of people was humbling.

During the lockdown, I discovered many medical student organizations, that were working to help those less privileged. I took on a project related to mental health, educating people and giving them a safe space to voice their fears.

In life, the greatest thing to do, is to help those who cannot help you.

In the midst of this, on teacher's day, during my third semester, I went to visit my teachers in the coaching centre. I have always been taught to acknowledge the role of all of my teachers in shaping me and helping me achieve my goal.

"How is it going Ananya?" my chemistry teacher asked.

"College is wonderful sir. We've started going to clinical postings now, but we don't have a lot of knowledge, so it isn't that enriching. Sometimes, it feels useless."

"If I were you, I would've followed my professors all day long" he said in reply.

A simple statement was such a huge eye-opener. I was where I always wanted to be, pursuing what I love. The first year of college I had complained of not being able to see patients and now I even had a chance to interact with them! I was fortunate to have the opportunity, and yet I wasn't making the best use of it. People cease to care for what they already have. On one such clinical rotation round, we were doing a customary physical exam on a young lady with complaints of breathlessness and palpitation. While checking the pulse, I noticed the rhythm was irregular, in contrast to the finding of my batch mates. On presenting my findings to the resident, she said, "She does have an irregular pulse. Well done."

I could've had an atrial flutter myself with the happiness of being able to recognize a clinical finding.

As our posting shifted from medicine to surgery, I met with yet another memorable patient. Around this time, our professors were teaching us that there is more to a patient than just their history. They were teaching us empathy, to listen to our patients, to visit them every day and ask them how they are, to build a rapport with them. It is essential to doctor-patient care, that the doctors are able to understand the pain the patient is going through, and that the patient trusts that their doctors are doing the best that they can.

Some weeks after this, my friends and I were taking the history of a middle aged gentleman who was present with his wife. I went to visit the patient again the next day, after going over through some of the points in the history. I asked them how they were doing. After I clarified some of the notes, I asked them if there was anything they needed. The wife with tears in her eyes told me that the doctors said her husband would be discharged today but there were still issues with his health. I felt helpless, but I listened to her, assured her that things would be alright, and promised to talk to the doctors about it.

When I reiterated her predicament to my professor, he pointed out an interesting fact.

"She doesn't know who you are, or your designation. All she saw is that someone in a white coat who talked to her husband yesterday, came to check on him today. She trusted you to tell you her problem. That's the responsibility of donning the white coat – you give an ear to people's pain and your actions can change someone's tears into a smile." At another time in my posting, I was going to get the attendance signed. I saw the doctors giving a patient cardiopulmonary resuscitation, and my heart stopped. I sucked in a breath and watched the scene unfold. The doctors were taking turns, with one palm folded over the other, trying to revive the patient. A portable curtain was covering them from everyone else. I waited and waited and waited. It felt like an eternity when they stopped. I released a shaky breath, and smiled. I turned to my friend and said, "they saved her"

"No, they didn't" he said.

"What?"

"She died" he said, pointing towards a man who was standing in front of a window. He had a phone to his ear, and was crying loudly.

I felt tears forming in my eyes. I rushed to the washroom, and took deep breaths. I was going to be a doctor; I should be able to handle my emotions especially when it's about life and death.

After a few seconds, or maybe minutes later, I returned.

"She did survive" my friend said to me.

"What?" I said again.

He pointed towards her bed, where I could see her shallow breathing. Oh my God, I thought.

"Were those tears of joy then?" I asked him.

"Or the pain of a near death experience" he replied.

For a doctor, diagnosing and curing are important skills, but the ability to be completely present with a patient and their families suffering, allowing the pain to change you, to help you grow – that is what we live for, that is what we become doctors for.

Vipra Kohli

Vipra is currently pursuing her 3rd professional year as a medic in Maharishi Markandeshwar Medical College and Hospital, Himachal Pradesh (India).

She values her surroundings and is like undying weed whose explosive power is awe-spring.

She believes that every individual has their own spark in the same way she is also full of mystic shine and shade.

She is curious to understand each new thing she catches on and has an artistic temperament. Vipra believes that happiness and opportunities are perfectly harmonized with our very own karma.

She thrives on the fact that people who are graced with the gift of sight, cannot unsee the truth and dwell into the darkness. Whether it is mixed media or digital she seeks to merge experiences into unified forms and believes that everyone is blessed with lion hearted courage, waiting to be explored!

CHAPTER 23

Invictus

Getting into a medical school was just a fantasy for me and yet, here I am!

As an average student in high school, I was never confident enough that I'll be pursuing a career as a medic, carrying out my distinct imagination.

This distinct imagination of mine was only possible, due to my parents' support and motivation. They always taught me to follow my dreams, work hard to make them true, and to be the sunshine for them.

My soul feared to take further steps after giving the board examinations, as in my high school days, it was not easy to pass due to my health issues. But being a follower of Nichiren Buddhism and keeping my mentor Daisaku Ikeda's words in mind, *"Even if the things don't unfold the way you expected, don't be disheartened or give up. One who continues to advance will win in the end"*, I strove with an ever-positive spirit as Champion of Challenges. I was determined to go to the college of my mission. With immense happiness, I stepped up, packed my bags, and immediately decided to start a new chapter of my life at *Maharishi Markandeshwar Medical College and Hospital, Solan* amidst the valley.

My journey started from the very first day of my orientation month. The embryonic days of the orientation were enthusiastic and amusing. We started with our hospital tours and learned about the basics of the 19 subjects we were going to study in five and a half years, which seemed interesting at the start- but soon we realized that the real journey of struggles was yet to begin.

My decision to study medicine was based on the fact that I hated physics, but soon I realized that there was *the* exhaustion of energy every single day just like thermodynamics. Our day would start by attending lectures sharp at 9, an endless flurry of classes, vivas, submissions, small group teachings, practicals, and a lot more. However, in front of my aim of becoming a humanistic doctor and in bringing a bigger impact in improving the health and wellness of people, these things were like salty peanuts. But whenever the salt was slightly excessive than normal, we would automatically go into a state of hypertension.

Although living in the hills was refreshing and chilling, the task to climb up the three mountains every day for 13 months was the foremost challenge. The three mountains were known as Anatomy, Physiology, and Biochemistry, our 1st professional subjects.

My seniors told me that anatomy was the toughest of all and eventually, I realized it too. It was one of the most important and difficult subjects, many used to fear it and I am not ashamed to say that I did too. Before every class, we were told that the knowledge of the anatomical structure of the body is basic to understand how both structure and function are modified by diseases and disorders- which is an important aspect of becoming a good doctor.

It was like the patron of 1st year and we were just slaves but the fun in the dissection hall and tears of Formalin is also one of the finest parts of medical school and is the moment when we actually realize that we are going to be doctors!

Well, the next hill was Physiology, the subject I hated the most. Everybody guided me to not learn physiology but to comprehend it. The physiology department was always the nasty one and their exams were always the crude ones.

But still, in the end, it is the most scoring one so eventually, there is a happy ending. The hardest hill to climb was Biochemistry. The misery came to us as budding doctors when we started studying metabolisms and performing practicals. These parts are a hardship for everyone and only *Satyanarayana* and *Md Rafi* helped us come out of this and pass with flying colors.

We 1ˢᵗ prof students too were affected by the pandemic. We had to understand and learn the half-term topics through online classes and realized the importance of dissection hall and lectures, we even missed being scolded by our teachers!

I realized that the strict rules of the hostel and the unerring attitude of the teachers kept us in pace and helped us focus on the destination rather than the journey. We escorted a disciplined schedule and enjoyed it to the fullest without compromising academics and our personal lives. This pandemic made me realize a lot about myself and made me question my existence, my purpose, and my responsibilities towards my family, friends, and nation.

From that moment I decided, *I'll be a new Vipra, a transformed version of myself, who will overcome all the shortcomings she had in her high school and initial months of college.* I decided to be part of various associations, took my responsibilities seriously, and built an impressive CV. I gained experience not only at the college level but was also internationally selected as a student delegate for an event (BRAINCOMS, Sau Paulo, Brazil).

I even pushed myself to the field of Research in Healthcare and Medical Education. The rule of processing an idea and executing it in the best way was a challenge but I decided to take it even though it was difficult as I never had a medical background.

My mentor Daisaku Ikeda says, *"Strive for extra 5 mins whenever you feel low or have* the feeling of giving up but never give up. *Strive to your hardest and the best will come from the universe".*

Keeping these words in my mind, I worked hard, sought my professors' help, consulted my colleagues, and attended webinars. My hard work paid off and I got the opportunity to become a part of clinical research.

In the end, I would like to conclude by saying do what not just makes you happy but also gives you a sense of satisfaction and sound sleep at the end of the day.

An important pro tip that I follow and guide my younger brother with is: the harder one strives to fulfill one's dreams, the unyielding results one gets!

Indraja Roy

An audacious girl willing to achieve her dreams , willing to help others through her kindest acts . She is a 22 year old Intern , from Gujarat studying at GCS Medical College . She is an enthusiastic human , likes to sketch , paint and read novels . Anatomy and pharmacology are her keen interest seeking subjects . Her continuous learning of nature from people , nature and other things always keeps her happy . Organizing and participating at events are one of her hobbies . Being down to earth and respecting every profession are her beliefs. She works on one rule , hard work betrays none , which helped her a lot in life .

CHAPTER 24

Journey of Infinite Possibilities

"A profession where knowledge, power, and heart come together. " This is something I firmly believe in. My story of medical school began at the age of eight, taking a stethoscope in one hand and wearing a white coat. I used to dream of becoming a doctor and used to play with these toys. The idea of treating people has fascinated me a lot.

This is the story of a series of experiences during the first year at my medical school.

Finally, the day arrived! It was the first day of my medical journey. A jumble of questions ran through my mind: *what will happen? How will it begin? Will it be tough?* Soon afterward, in between such thoughts, we were told to head towards our biochemistry labs. That was our first learning class of the day. We headed straight towards it. New day, new experiences, new place; it was going to be a wonderful experience. I was so nervous and unfortunately, I was the odd one out. Guess how? Because I, in a hurry, did a stupid thing and forgot my white coat. Adrenaline rushed through my body. My professor, being strict, was annoyed and scolded me for the fallacy. I never knew I could feel so much pain but I motivated myself and apologized for the mistake.

Yes, I know this is such a tiny thing but it was the first day and the idea of making a good first impression was a failure. It was such an embarrassing moment for me. I never expected such a thing could happen. I attended the class but was unable to pay attention because the series of events were continuously replaying in my mind.

Now, time for the second class came. It was physiology. Nobody could imagine what a strict and tough beginning it was. Our professor taught us some instruments and told us to draw them up. We set out to complete the task. After finishing, he asked us to show it to him, and soon, it was my turn. And now again I was broken because he, while checking, asked me to walk out of the department just because I forgot to draw a simple line and he said that there was no correction to be done in class. Tears rushed through my eyes and I lost all hope.

I decided to quit medical school because it was so tough. All my dreams were like pieces of broken glass. Small small bad incidents broke my dedication and as the place was new, I had nobody to share my day and bad experiences with. I went home and shared the same with my mother and told her that I wanted to quit medical school but she told me to sit and explained to me that success is no accident, it is hard work, perseverance, learning, studying, and sacrifice.

You won't get success easily. And, as mothers are the root of everyfoundation, she planted the seed of hard work in my mind. I decided not to lose hope.

The next morning, I was so excited for a new, refreshing start- thinking that no matter how bad the beginning, maybe it will be a great journey ahead. With enthusiasm, in a proper, well-ironed white coat I was ready for every task. I attended all the lectures and then headed towards the anatomy hall. It was so shocking to see cadavers laying over tables. It was scary but interesting to see.

Our ma'am taught us about muscles and the upper limb and gave us a task in which we all had to explain some topics in a given time duration in front of the whole class. I was so nervous and I was just preparing myself to give that presentation. I prayed to God that I shouldn't create any blunder. Hearing the applause for other colleagues made me a bit more nervous.

Suddenly the name "Indraja Roy" struck my ears. Suddenly attentive, I walked towards the projector and started giving my presentation. *My ma'am praised me and said it was nice and well done.* She told others also to be clearer and give the presentation as I did.

It was a victory for me. I felt as if I had achieved something so big. After all, small victories make up a big one. In my head, I thought, *sometimes when things are falling apart, they may actually be falling into place. The past experiences didn't break me, instead, they made me strong.* I wasn't ready for half of the bad incidents I went through but obviously; I was built for it.

I was self-confident and working harder each passing day. I gave my hundred percent in every task and my love for medical school increased. *It doesn't matter what's written in your story so far, it's how you fill-up the rest of the pages that counts.*

Mohit Jain

Mohit Jain, currently in his final year of MBBS at Seth GS Medical College and KEM Hospital, has been penning down his musings in the form of thought-provoking poems and write ups since he was in the 8th grade. The dream to become a sane doctor and an insane writer keeps him going. He has been a part of the college symposium team that was honored to give presentations and win at various platforms. He is actively involved in a few research studies at his teaching hospital. As a writer, his entries have been awarded in a couple of writing competitions. Being a sympathetic ear his interests are not just limited to medical books, but also encompass literature, storytelling, history, philosophy, politics and psychology, and one can never feel short of topics to strike a real conversation with him.

CHAPTER 25

You Don't Belong

"You don't belong." Ever had that voice in your head telling you how unworthy you are of sharing the same space as others? I did. Multiple times. I have felt it in my chest and I have felt it in my bones. Sometimes, I go on with life despite it being there. At others, it has consumed my days. Scientists call it by many names including imposter syndrome, impostorism, imposter experience, imposter phenomenon, and fraud syndrome. I believed in it like a fact for a very long time.

I have been lucky enough to strike conversations with people who are way smarter than me in certain aspects of life, share first experiences with people who have been doing it for a long time, and listen to people who seemed to have it all figured out. I thought to myself that "You don't belong" because that felt true in all logical sense. I tried to console myself in various ways - "the feelings will go away", "you are here for a reason" or at times been in an "I just don't care" mood. I am even guilty of belittling my first world problems when things are blowing up around us.

I even fantasized that if I hustle hard enough, maybe I will grow enough to belong. But as I climbed to higher rungs of the ladder, the feeling was still there. (Also, you will never stop finding people who are better than you in some sense or the other - my apologies if I am stating the obvious.) Even high achievers share this curse. Despite being a big name, Einstein was plagued with self-doubt: *The exaggerated esteem in which my life work is held makes me very ill at ease. I feel compelled to think of myself as an involuntary swindler,"* he told a friend. So, a higher degree of achievement is not the solution to overcoming these feelings.

We live through this life making a set of assumptions - assumptions about others and assumptions about ourselves. Assumptions telling us that others have earned it through hard work, while we are merely a wild card. We have an idea about who we are and where we belong. When we land up in unfamiliar circumstances, our very beliefs about ourselves are challenged. So we protect them as well as we possibly can, often at the expense of our peace and sanity. We choose to suffer rather than changing our beliefs because it feels like a much better and safer option.

We must learn to be better to ourselves, by letting go of our assumptions - for holding on is just self-sabotage.

I do not have the answers for everyone who feels like an imposter. Although something that has helped me personally is diving into the deep end of these beliefs with people I trust. Be vulnerable about what you feel and try to explore why. Maybe they might offer a new perspective. It's tiring to be ironclad, so share a few chinks in your armor. Odds are you might even find someone who has felt the same way at some point or another. It seems a little less daunting to go on then, a little more at peace. That's not to say that your story isn't special, rather be grateful that it's not. Whatever hardship you might have to deal with, you are never alone.

Chosen Family -

I never thought that a family could exist outside of a home,

But surely are we a family, without a common womb,

We came together by chance, but stay together by choice,

All mute in our own ways, together we found a voice.

Like parts of an aircraft riveted together with emotions,

We navigated both clear skies and heavy commotions,

Even with differing opinions about love, lust, and life,

Empathizing over others' reference points is how we thrive.

Although not always, for at times we barely survive,

Unknowingly often pushing someone to the edge,

Wise enough to quickly lend a hand to fetch, to safety from the ledge.

Evolved in ways inconceivable with members missing,

We keep each other in check through critiquing and listening.

Our roots are vital, but why would we choose despair over rejoice?

We came together by chance and we stayed together by choice.

Code Blue -

It was just another day at the wards,

Averagely paced and loud - regular in all sense,

We solicited a doctor on his regular shift,

To enlighten us a little, with his knowledge immense,

He agreed, we cheered as he demonstrated signs from patient to patient,

As we examined the third one, quickly did things get tense.

From alert, to drowsy, to limp she went,

Saturations dropped as breathing no longer remained spontaneous;

As the doctor called the nurse for help,

We backed up, trying to comprehend the tyrannous situation.

Chaos, it seemed to the lay, and even to us -

Despite knowing there are protocols to trust,

The doctor, though, swiftly went through the motions,

In, as I recall, the silent commotion.

A life was saved, by brains and hands calloused,

All while a man shouted at a woman for being callous,

She began to cry, in confusion, panic, and guilt;

We decided to leave figuring out there was nothing more the doctor could tell us.

First time did I experience firsthand how quickly life can turn,

And the first time I saw a human pull back another from the point of no return -

I am still in awe of that day,

When life, at once, jumped over the fence,

It was just another day at the wards,

Rapidly paced and loud - regular in all sense.

Shirish Rao

A final year MBBS student at Seth GS Medical College & KEM Hospital, mastering his academics with straight 'A's & winning numerous state & national level quizzes, he manages to maintain a perfect balance between academics, co-curriculars and community service.

His endless passion for research with the purpose of making a difference in the society has led to the foundation of various projects and programs. Showcasing exceptional problem solving and leadership skills, he has organized multiple events & presently serves as the Sr. Secretary of ASPIRE.

In his free time, he enjoys hanging out with friends, going on treks & playing guitar.

CHAPTER 26

Don't Be Your Own Bottleneck

Waking up to a new day, touring through different departments, checking up with IEC regarding the approval of my new projects, spending a few hours in the library polishing my concepts, cycling back to the hostel, finishing off an online class with my student at VECTOR, just another day in my dynamic life was coming to an end. With the college finally reopening in the next two days & the University exams being 2 months away, I sit back & look at the year gone by.

It was August 2019; I was about to enter the second year of my Med school on the back of a year which I felt couldn't have been any better. I had already won 4 quizzes, been part of an amazing 'Aavishkaar' & made a bunch of wonderful friends. I was looking at it as a year filled with new challenges & opportunities. I was still wondering if I should get into some kind of research? Organize some event in Aavishkaar? Be a part of Alfaaz again? Continue volunteering for VECTOR? Or just focus on my academics & participate in a few more quizzes?

The year started with me flying off to Indonesia with my team for the Inter-Medical School Physiology Quiz. From standing 1st among 100 international universities in the written round to making such silly mistakes in the Quarterfinals only to end up 14th, the journey was no less than a rollercoaster ride.

Soon after returning to the college, my endless passion for research found Symposium as the grandest platform to learn, conduct & present not just research but also formulate strategies & solutions for the under-addressed medico-social issues. In a team filled with some awesome, enthusiastic people, I managed to find my place as a Researcher. Brainstorming ideas, touring departments, preparing & getting our proposal approved & visiting schools, colleges & housing societies across Mumbai, our project to determine the prevalence, causes, & health implications of Screen Overuse & Addiction has been a journey of its own kind, throughout which we were also able the serve the community through seminars and our website. From understanding my abilities as a Researcher who formed the backbone of all our projects, to taking up responsibilities as the Team leader, Symposium has been the thing that brought the most out of me.

While our projects were under the IEC review for a month, my love for dancing 'crazily', pulled me back to Alfaaz Dance. It doesn't really matter how bad you are at something if doing it gives you that joy, that happiness & that 'carefree moment', go for it. From being no less than a dancing clown to dancing as one of the leads in the front row, would always be at the top tons of wonderful memories that we, as 'Alfaaz Family' shared between us.

Somewhere around the same time, I, the Jr. The Academic Secretary got involved in another event of Aavishkaar- Model United Nations. Given how naïve I was, my first ever experience at organizing turned out to be an eye-opener in many aspects. Being a part of an organizing team is no less than the typical political scenario of India, the only difference being that Indian politics is still far more democratic. Looking towards the brighter side, I did get to learn a lot about approaching sponsors, handling finances, microplanning & on day event management. Putting our differences aside we stuck together as a team and managed to pull off a very successful, first-ever GSMUN.

Amidst the lockdown, the entire symposium work was put on hold. My term as the Jr. Academic Secretary was over, and then came the Senior Gymkhana interviews, providing me an opportunity which I still feel was the best amongst everything I have ever done. I was selected as the Sr. Secretary of ASPIRE, the Student's Research Council of Seth GSMC. I along with my Co-Secretary, starting as a team of two have now put together a family for more than 50 working members, who have put their hearts out through lockdown to bring ASPIRE to a level that we take pride in. From conducting multiple Research Methodology workshops, talks & monthly journal clubs to compiling A to Z resources to learn research & creating a Research Guidance Community on Discord, today ASPIRE stands with a reputation of its own and a reach of over 5000 medical students & doctors across its social media platforms, which is also the reason behind ASPIRE being the official outreach partner of this very book.

Managing extra-curricular activities along with academics has been a tough task, & has taken an equal toll on my body & mind. For this very reason, a majority of students choose the easier way of just focusing on their academics & ultimately never come out of their bubble. I would say- if not all, but everyone must get involved in at least something, if not, then at least don't second guess yourself when your friends invite you for a trip, party, or any other fun activity. One can only learn to swim if he gathers enough courage to at least jump into the pool. From what I have seen & experienced, the key to finding the right balance is working with deadlines, prioritizing things & understanding how much & what kind of knowledge or experience is enough for you. The very first thing that we need to unlearn is competing with & comparing ourselves to others. Everyone is built differently & has their own purpose & ways of leading their lives. Realizing our strengths, we find that the only one whom we need to compete with is who we were yesterday & build the self whom we wish to be tomorrow.

"Lack of confidence kills more dreams than the lack of abilities. You are capable of much more than you realize. Don't be your own bottleneck". With this little piece of motivation, I rock back on my chair with a satisfied smile on my face, awaiting my friends return, awaiting the approval of my new research projects, awaiting college to start & finally awaiting more opportunities that would guide my way into a career in research to make me capable enough to bring about a change in today's world.

Mihir Joshi

This is Mihir M Joshi. He is a 2nd year student, studying MBBS in MGM medical college, Aurangabad.

He is currently working on a case report paper on ' Spontaneous intracranial hypotension and associated cranial neuropathies ' .

He likes to seize every opportunity that comes his way, and he always likes to work hard for what he believes in.

He likes helping people.

His hobbies include singing, playing drums, listening to music and audiobooks, and traveling.

He is very passionate about being a doctor, as he thinks that if he can change even 1 life for the better, it will all be worth it.

CHAPTER 27

The Hardest Part

"Please someone call the doctor!" he screamed as he hit the brake,

"Oh, doctor please check my mother for God's sake!".

Covered in a PPE kit, the doctor emerged all in white,

The son saw him in his shining armor as if he was his knight.

"Please do something doctor," he urged with all his might,

The doctor checked his mother, his expression as dark as the night.

"Please have a seat," the doctor said,

"Oh God, give me the strength to break this news to him!" he prayed.

"Why are you asking me to sit at the doctor, don't you see my mother is in pain?"

He looked at the doctor as if he was insane.

Inside the doctor, all the emotions swirled,

As his next words are going to collapse someone's whole world.

"There is no easy way to say this... the doctor swore,

"But unfortunately, your mother is no more..."

"But she was talking to me an hour ago!" the son burst into tears,

"This can't be true!" he still couldn't believe his ears.

The doctor felt a strange sense of despair,

Because all he could do was stare,

At the son's worst nightmare.

He had to do this, it was a part of his job, he knew from the start,

20 years working as a doctor, but this was always the Hardest part...

Shruti D Bhakare

This is Shruti D Bhakare 2nd year MBBS student studying at Dr D.Y Patil Medical college, Navi Mumbai. She loves exploring new things. She can speak french. She has presented her research work in FIRMST (Forum for Interdisciplinary Research in Medical Science and Technology) and Medinspire. Her research has been published in " The Physician journal of The British Association of Physicians of Indian Origin".

Shruti wants to become a doctor to be able to help people who are in pain and agony, as seeing people in pain is one thing she can't stand.

CHAPTER 28

A Face That is Always Smiling

"Don't go to the doctor, they just write a medicine and charge a fortune, try this remedy I saw on Whatsapp instead"

The patient is brought to the doctor in a critical condition but when the doctor can't save the patient, the doctor is brutally beaten and the hospital is vandalized. The doctor is treated the way a criminal should be treated, all for just trying to save his/her patient's life.

"These allopathy medicines which these doctors give have a lot of side effects you know"

The patient will ask you if the drug you are prescribing him/her has many side effects and some of them won't even take the medicine, because they have side effects. Then the same people will go and smoke packs of cigarettes and chug bottles of alcohol like its green tea. Do they ask if the pack of cigarettes or the bottle of alcohol have any side effects? I don't think so.

This is not a rant; this is just the point of view of a medico after all the books' title is 'World through a stethoscope isn't it?'

So, it's time for you to step into our shoes, wearing which, we have walked thousands of miles down a long and weary road. Let's see, if you can fit your feet...

When you say we just charge a fortune for just touching you and writing a prescription, have you ever wondered how much we have trained ourselves to diagnose your pain by just a touch? Have you seen us googling the names of the medicines before we prescribe for you? No, right? It is this knowledge that we charge for.

When you beat a doctor for not saving your relative or friend do you ever think whether what you are doing makes any sense in the slightest? You just expect that the doctor will pull out a magic wand, chant a spell, and voila the patient gets up and goes home.

Well let me ask all my medico friends a question, has anyone of you or anyone you know of has completed his/her M.B.B.S. from Hogwarts?

No? I thought so...

Please try to understand that the doctor is also a human being like everybody else,

A human being who is doing his best to save the patient.

Even after all of this,

A doctor always fulfills his duties.

A doctor never refuses treatment to a patient.

A doctor stays on duty for twenty-four hours if needed.

A doctor has to go through a long and rigorous process to become what he is today.

He has to endure countless sleepless nights.

A doctor is always late to all his family functions, and has to keep his loved ones waiting, because for the doctor his/her patient is their first priority.

A doctor has to keep his knowledge up to date with this ever-evolving world of science.

A doctor answers your phone calls and takes your follow-ups even when he is on a vacation or a holiday. He is always on duty.

But the most important thing that you might not have noticed is...

No matter what the doctor has been through or no matter how the doctor feels he always greets you with a warm smile on his face.

I am and will always be proud to be a medico.

Aditya Bihani

Aditya Shailesh Bihani is an Enthusiastic Medical Student, studying 3rd Year MBBS Course at H.B.T. Medical College and Dr. R. N. Cooper Mun. Gen. Hospital, Juhu, Mumbai. He is a diligent person with a Never-say-die attitude. He is an active member of LIFT FOR UPLIFTMENT ORGANIZATION, a platform, which helps in Educating and Guiding the Needy but aspiring Medicos, preparing for NEET-UG Exam. He has participated in the Pulse Polio immunization Drives, Health Camps organized for BEST and Other Municipal Corporation employees, Health Education and Awareness Drives in the community. Currently, he is working as COVID Warrior at Municipal Corporation of Greater Mumbai, Mumbai. He has successfully helped in triaging COVID positive patients. He is a responsible individual with a positive attitude and a broad vision. His goal is to work on Ease of Accessibility of Health Care for Everyone.

CHAPTER 29

Tackling Pandemonium Of The Pandemic

Describing a Doctor's Journey in Words,

Is like, in an endless sky, counting the Birds.

When the entire Nation was under Lockdown,

The Doctor had put on his Protective Gown.

I see the globe; wearing an apron white,

In this pandemic how bravely medicos fight!

Through the stethoscope, the sounds of the world I hear,

Of people's Confusion, Anxiety, Stress, and Fear.

It was doctors and team handling the Pandemonium,

While everyone else was comfortable in their Condominium.

The role of the medical fraternity has been Pivotal,

In pandemic prevention, care, diagnosis, treatment, and In total.

Medicine is a profound science that cultivates clinical skills, knowledge, and social values, shaping you into a compassionate clinician and an exemplary human being. Sacrifices are inherent in this field—sleep, leisure, meals, holidays, time with loved ones, personal health, and at times, even lives. From the early days of my MBBS journey, I actively engage in health camps and community programs. However, this year's Pulse Polio Immunization Drive presented unique challenges. The overstressed medical facilities and burdened fraternity demanded utmost precautions and adherence to COVID protocols. Interacting with Community Health Volunteers and Paramedical Staff, I trained them on vaccinating children safely. These individuals work tirelessly at the community level, ensuring the implementation of health schemes devised at the highest level.

While the entire world is still struggling with the *Sars-Cov-2 Novel Corona Virus Infectious Disease*, it is the pandemonium rather than the pandemic which has troubled people more! The entire world, initially could not understand the nature of the disease, the spread of the disease, the manner of spread, the complications, and the people at high risk. To add more to the people's confusion, there were fake messages on social media. The entire situation was chaotic. I felt that dealing with the chaos was equally important as dealing with the disease. The need for a system for resolving people's doubts was unavoidable. I, being a man of medicine, wanted to contribute somehow to society. And there it was! I got an opportunity to work as a COVID warrior as an Undergraduate MBBS student at *the Municipal Corporation of Greater Mumbai*. The nature of work is:

- Triaging COVID-19 Patients.
- Tele-counseling of positive patients.
- Counseling of the patients' relatives.
- Bed Management and Hospitalization of symptomatic patients and Isolation of asymptomatic patients.
- Arranging ambulances to shift patients to isolation facilities/ hospitals.

- Guiding the relatives of critically ill patients about various modalities available For Plasma Therapy.
- Tracing high-risk contacts of positive patients.
- Helping people to overcome myths and fear regarding COVID-19.
- Guiding people regarding the protocols for COVID Deaths.
- Daily follow up of patients who opt-to Home Isolation.
- Assisting people's queries regarding traveling/containment zones/sanitation of residence.

In the midst of COVID-19, my responsibilities extended beyond office work, including the challenging task of persuading patients to isolate. Addressing the stigma and debunking prevalent myths surrounding the virus proved difficult. Some patients, living in cramped spaces and using shared facilities, were reluctant to shift to isolation centers. With the help of the police, we had to convince them for their own well-being and that of the community. Many patients denied their COVID-positive status, despite experiencing symptoms. Unfortunately, during August-September, Mumbai faced a severe shortage of medical facilities. It was disheartening to inform patients that their preferred beds were unavailable due to high occupancy. Even jumbo facilities struggled to accommodate patients. Thankfully, collective efforts improved the situation. Patient appreciation messages, like one saying, "Thanks a billion, billion," served as motivation to work harder for the community. COVID screening camps for essential service employees, such as BEST and Municipal Corporation staff, were crucial. Despite being symptomatic and isolating as a high-risk contact, I tested negative. I express gratitude to the doctors who assisted with bed management. As a medical student, I believe I played a small but significant role in raising awareness and managing the pandemic. This is just the beginning of a long journey, with many more milestones to achieve. Medicine requires sacrifices and the integration of theoretical knowledge and clinical skills.

Doctor working day and Night,

In the pandemic blight.

May you gather courage more,

The people of you proudly roar!

Anushree Rai

The first doctor in the family hierarchy, Anushree Rai found her solace and peace in striving towards becoming a meticulous and empathetic doctor. She is passionately pursuing medicine and surgery and is currently in her 4th professional year. She has continued to empower future healthcare professionals in the capacity of an Executive board member of a leading Medical Student Organization in India. Apart from her work as a global health advocate, she is also volunteering in various organizations that work for climate change and diversity, equity and Inclusion (DEI). A graceful dancer and Debating enthusiast, she never stops trying to be the best version of herself and aspires to become an Interventional Radiologist in the near future!

My Journey Towards Healthcare Advocacy And Empowering Future Physicians

Health advocacy is widely known today for changing, keeping, and improving pieces of legislation that deal with healthcare. it's going to also affect promoting health and access to healthcare in communities. But how can a medical student's voice be so important in addressing health equities? And why should we already add even more to our already full plate where books, exams, and clinical rotations seem more important to our rigid minds?

For me, the journey of finding a voice and the interest in advocating it all started when I joined the one of the leading medical student associations in India, Asian Medical Students' Association (Indian Chapter). I realized the vastness of potential that medicos possess and by that I do not mean just academically, but with respect to leadership and health advocacy. As an adept Member of the Executive Board, I came across some amazing opportunities and a lot of fellow aspiring medical students which taught about how important is that our voices be heard, whether it be for controversial bills or even decision making amidst the pandemic.

We (me and fellow medicos at AMSA-India) were all trying our best to swim across what's called the ocean of knowledge, and yet each one of us had our own stories of courage and beyond. However, what really made us work and rejoice our little wins together was the purpose, the purpose to lead and empower medical students with the triune of knowledge, friendship and action.

Moving forward as to why health advocacy matters?.. is because it isn't just important, it's imperative since all the disparities and injustices are at their heart. There are many various sorts of advocacy, but what 's important to know is that you simply are engaging in activism for particular issues and are actively being involved so as to influence people about these issues.

As a medico, you'll begin to include advocacy and health equity into your curriculum. Having the ability to interact and study pressing issues within the world and connecting them to your classes, or your rotations will allow you to ascertain the larger picture of why advocacy is important to be a well-rounded physician.

You'll be ready to understand diseases on a special level and even your patient's lifestyle choices or medical record. You'll realize that someone's chronic health issues are often the result of the shortage of accessible healthy food or doctors' offices in their rural community. You'll change it by advocating for this. This is often exactly why advocacy as a medico is so important. You'll rally and advocate for change within the community to provide more doctors or healthy food options.

Now that I have even mentioned tools and efforts of advocating health, what about topics? To supply a clearer view on an equivalent, there are innumerable topics you'll start with. Some substantial of them being, social determinants of health, psychological state, global climate change effects on the physical body and lastly the unwanted strenuous working hours that we are expected to figure in. And there's such a lot more than I haven't listed thanks to the constraint of words. For e.g. I'm hooked on psychological state and felt how the stigma around it made it harder for patients or maybe loved ones to share their experiences! So, I have been involved in psychological state advocacy since I used to be 16. And still do advocacy efforts till today!

Remember, all the samples of advocacy are great ways to urge your feet wet, but to possess efficient grassroots advocacy you would like to teach and rally up people and check out to possess a permanent change in your community.

Write a letter to the editor, hold awareness sessions, write columns, organize campaigns, start a petition, or maybe just join which medical student organization suits you the best and just don't limit yourself to the knowledge in books. We medical students have an influential voice that must be exercised to form our communities, our country, and quite frankly, the planet a far better place, to which this year was a testimony. Activism will fire a passion within you to continue practicing medicine in a way you've never felt before. I promise you. Advocate for your past, present, and future patients. Advocate for your own community. Lastly, altogether of that, the foremost important thing I even have learned while working in various medical non-governmental organizations is that we are in a unique position to assist and it's our duty, as aspiring physicians, to try to do just that.

Anu Saroa

Anu Saroa is a final year M.B.B.S student . She is very enthusiastic about writing and literature. She wants to heal the world with the power of a pen. She believes that writing is a good way of expressing oneself.

CHAPTER 31

The Indelible Experience

"Ah! such an indelible memory of my first clinical posting in the surgery department. Donning the white coat, eyes brimming with joy. It was early October, probably, I remember. We were all sitting on our benches in the demo room. Our luminary Professor entered the room. They are the sun of knowledge in the realm of surgery. We were asked to open the *"A Manual on Clinical Surgery by S.Das"* and read about the "Examination of Lump ". We were reading when our Professor started discussing the questions pertaining to the topic, leading to a strong discussion.

Then came the time of putting knowledge into skills. The inexperience into experience. We all were naive. But the support of knowledge was empowering. That lucky day, it was my turn for history taking. An old man with a lump on his neck entered the room. We offered him a seat to sit. He would have been a very poor and feeble man. His wisdom was the only staff of his age.

"Roll no. 12 and 14, please continue with your history taking," said our professor. I went forward and asked him his name and all the particulars. Throughout history, I realized one thing- he was a laborer by occupation. He told us that he was a laborer and he came from a distant village, mostly from a rural area. He was sharing all his sorrows and providing us details about the lump- when did it arise, duration, other symptoms of the lumps. The crux from the discourse was that I realized there was a pain in his sorrow. There was pain in his pain. Though, being professional, I was touched by the story. He was so generous and although it was painful, he allowed every student in the batch to touch and palpate his lump on his neck. After history taking was over, my batchmate and I were writing and preparing the history to present it before our professor. In the meantime, my mind was ruminating over his story. He was joining his hands before every student and saying "You all are doing a great job. Study and serve people. I know the importance of study." His generosity and cooperative attitude towards doctors gave me an immense sense of responsibility.

A teacher is a candle who burns themselves to give the light of knowledge to others. I regard that person to be a teacher in my professional life and personal life. He taught me three lessons of life:

1. A doctor has a huge responsibility for not only curing people but also changing their lives.
2. The power of empathy and being a skillful doctor.
3. Every experience and moment teaches us a wonderful lesson.

I still remember I asked my class fellow to read the history and present before the entire class. Our professor appreciated us and then we all were discussing the probable diagnosis for the above case. My professor was so humble and kind in his conversation with that patient that I decided to be a gentle and humble doctor too. I vowed to myself that I will give my fullest and treat everyone with full skill and a good attitude.

This incident in my life has affected me personally and professionally. *"Pain is inevitable. But suffering is a choice."* I think that we should serve our Country and help as many people as we can.

Varsha John

Varsha John is a third year medical student, a diehard bibliophile , enthusiastic about writing and an animal lover.

She is also passionate about medicine and hopes to be a pediatrician in the future.

Her strong love for books opened the doorway to attempt to spin her own stories and through WTAS she is taking her baby steps to be a published author.

CHAPTER 32

A Lesson For Life

The first day of medical school was the day it finally hit me: that at the end of the long run, I would be a doctor! A lifelong dream.

Of course, it doesn't sound as simple as that. Through the three years of medical school (I'm in my third year now), life was jam-packed: with projects, case reports, homework, and exams, with cultural and college fests, practical works, and a ginormous amount to study.

It was like any other university life. Except in the back of my mind, in a small teeny- tiny space of my brain, there was the gnawing awareness that I was dealing with patients. Real people. With feelings, dreams, and aspirations of their own, now in a hospital for various reasons. A place that was brimming with knowledge and wisdom for us medical students but was probably a giant pot of hope and despair in equal measures for the people seeking our care – the patients.

Awareness that the best book for your study, the best reference is a real person, is a bit daunting. Nevertheless, it is true. The person who would help you become a good doctor is your patient. Over the course of three years in medical school, after countless rotations in multiple departments and seeing, meeting, and taking cases of various patients, I have come to realize that there are many lessons that one can learn. Apart from the signs and symptoms, the various presenting complaints and investigations a lesson that I have learned is an untold one: the power of empathy.

Empathy is putting yourself in someone else's shoes. Seeing what they see, feeling what they feel. It gives an entirely different perspective of situations. Of all the patients that I have met, talked to, and taken cases of to present them, one of them really taught me this lesson.

He was an old man, admitted to the general ward due to chronic cough and hemoptysis.

His bystander was his wife. They were all alone. I was assigned the case for my exam. An exam looming in the corner definitely dampens your spirit. You just want to get over it as fast as possible. I was trying to extract some history from this gentleman about his chief complaints, swallowing my own nervousness, but he had other plans. He insisted on talking about his family and children and his home, about his youth when he was a strong man needing nobody's care and help. When he realized that I was in the middle of an exam, he did give me a detailed colorful history, but not before he and his wife offered me breakfast, tea, and fruits.

It wasn't until the viva was over that I realized that probably my patient- who warmly offered me food, soothed my nerves before the viva, and who was a really sweet old man- was just lonely.

Maybe his attempts to engage me in conversation, his attempts to recollect his past when he was strong and healthy, were just his unhappiness and realization of being reduced to just another patient in the huge ward, at the mercy of the medical staff and not the strong farmer he once was, tilling his land and seeing his fruits grow.

Putting myself in his place made me conscious that while for me, the important thing was to identify and elicit the signs and symptoms, and give a differential diagnosis, life looked a little different for him. It was in all likelihood filled with worry about his illness and his finances, but also with trust and hope in his doctors and nurses. It must have been like a crossroad, where you are forced to remember your past and your choices, and wonder if you have a future to do things you wanted to.

That day I realized that while we as medical students crowd around the patients, inspecting and palpating them, discussing excitedly about identified signs, appreciating the various breath sounds and heart sounds and reflexes, every minute of their waking lives was equivalent to a lone warrior fighting an unpredictable battle in a far of land. Maybe their heart sounds did not have murmurs, but it was probably heavy all the same at the prospect of what they were facing.

I visited my patient after the exam for the rest of the days until he was discharged. We talked a great deal. It was new to me. Being an introvert, making conversations with people I didn't know well, did not come easily. But he was happy, and I realized, so was I. It was wonderful to pass by his bed and say a hi, to again be offered tea and biscuits and what not and talk about agriculture, a subject I sadly was not well-versed in, but was quickly learning. We quickly became friends with the occupants of the next bed as well. It struck me how they drew comfort from each other, how they kept each other's hopes raised. A lot of times, I realized, they just wanted assurance. That the sun would shine again on the horizon, and flowers would bloom afresh.

A hospital is not a place where you would hope to meet again. So when he got discharged, I was in equal parts happy and sad. Happy that he was well and could go back to the life that he had left behind. Sad because I was going to miss him.

Even though, as predicted, I haven't seen him again, he left behind an Alibaba's cave full of memories and lessons. Something that I won't forget for the rest of the years.

My journey through medical school is still filled to the brim with numerous things to be done. Yet each day in class, each patient whose case I need to take, I'm reminded of the untold lesson taught. I'm reminded that being a doctor is more than just wearing a white coat and carrying a stethoscope.

As Hippocrates rightly said: *"Wherever the art of medicine is loved, there is also a love of humanity."*

Nirosha Susan Mathew

She just wants to maintain her sanity by pouring her thoughts onto a paper as it is getting crammed up in her mind.

CHAPTER 33

MBBS - Behind The Scenes

"Throw some scrubs on

Put your hair up

Drink some coffee

And handle it."

The aforementioned words have been credited to an anonymous source on the internet that aptly describes the expectations, as well as provides a piece of advice to survive medical life.

For it is not meant for the fainthearted or weak-willed to wage a battle against lakhs of aspiring students to secure a medical seat. Then we continue with the rigorous trials and training designed to expose the naive future doctors to a tiny glimpse of their future. And rigorous it has to be, as a doctor is a god but at the same time could easily be at the receiving end of slaps and beatings for failing to defy God and nature itself. Rightly so! After all, a doctor is a god in disguise who is obliged to save humanity and not a mere human who is also somebody's son.

Clad in white overalls treading the halls of D- hall to the day when you first adorn your scrubs it simply seems like a bittersweet dream. It's ironic that I mention dreams, as we forgo our precious sleep with cups of coffee to memorize diseases and their drugs. Again, ironic I mention drugs as medical students tend to abuse these same drugs to keep our eyes from shutting after a day of running through wards and reciting history taking and being scolded for doing it incorrectly as what awaits us in our dorms are books as heavy as bricks and fonts as small as a legume. Again, ironically I mention legumes as the legume curry in our mess will be completely dearth of legumes and be more like a soup. Talk of being in a soup!

Okay enough with the word trickery but describing medical life is quite hard as it is not just made of big moments but of tiny minuscule moments too which would require microscopes. The unforgettable memories with friends and girlfriends, friendly ragging with seniors and juniors, realization that it is basically a hub of nerds who are sick of studying and that there is a hidden Hrithik Roshan in each one of us after two sips of cheap Corona. But when we enter our shrine, the hospital, we leave it all behind, the hangover, the heartbreak, or the hardship of just being a twenty- something student and focus on understanding the concepts, try to keep up with the best of the country, and also not offend our insanely strict professors. Yes, it is quite a mountain on our overall-clad backs. Passing exams is the hurdle, not the marks. From 99% to 60%, the fall is a kick to your ego and confidence but the only thing keeping you on track is the hundreds of others who are in the same boat or could be even drowning. New meanings of friendships and co-dependence evolve where your family seems distant but these sleep-deprived fellow students become more than family. You grow, both physically and emotionally, seeing pain in a whole new light and appreciating the worth of a warm embrace over gold any day.

We may not remember the words inscribed on our books but we do remember the agony in the eyes or wails of each patient. We remember our scoldings and tears and desperation. Also, the lonely nights with books by our side feeling the weight of the world trying not to lose hope and begin studying again hoping for a better tomorrow.

Exams seem like a combined effort both outside and inside examination halls. Each student knows something the other doesn't and during exam season we become like a battalion, concerned for ourselves but also praying not to leave a man behind.

From fainting in D halls to cutting open a live human, a doctor takes birth. They say doctors are competitive freaks but I feel with the number of competitive exams that have been set in a medical journey, it would be a miracle if that toxic competitiveness didn't seep into a medico's brain. From USMLE to PLAB to NEXT these uppercase words become the starring heroes (or villains) of our lives.

And please don't forget all this burden is along with the gruesome teenage years filled with growth spurts and hormonal changes. Your skin breaks along with your heart.

So, when you see a doctor, remember there are a thousand of seen and unseen efforts, multiple sleepless nights filled with incessant praying, and an abundance of fun-filled memories as well.

Madhulika Kotiyal

Madhulika stumbled into the world of medicine in 2016 and since then has been treading this long , arduous, yet fulfilling path of becoming a doctor. She can weave a few lines whenever Creativity knocks on her door. She also wishes to write articles for newspapers and magazines in the future. (Maybe pen down a novel, once she stops procrastinating!)

Along with writing, she also wants to use her experiences as Doctor, not only to treat people but also understand their quirks and uniqueness.

She's currently pursuing MBBS from Government Doon Medical College, Dehradun. She aspires to pursue a career in Paediatric Surgery.

CHAPTER 34

How Medicine Changed Me As A Person

As I'm at the cusp of finishing my MBBS degree, I often reflect on the days when I couldn't even imagine or rather, dreaded the idea of becoming a doctor. Yes, my reader, you've read it right! *I dreaded the idea of becoming a doctor.* So, you might be wondering, how on the earth did she land in this field?

For that, I'll have to take you a bit back in time when I was preparing for my entrance examinations.

Since my childhood, I have been wandering around my career choice; one day an astronaut, another day a chef. This list is long. Eventually, molecular biology caught my fancy and I thought, 'This seems interesting. I want to pursue this!'. The idea of becoming a molecular biologist excited me more as I was a complete introvert. All I needed was a good laboratory and I won't have to interact with humanity ever! That was my Grand Design to live with my introverted self. I prepared for JEE and NEET simultaneously, hoping to get admission into the Indian Institute of Science, Bangalore, and pursue B.Sc in Biology.

However, as our elders have said, 'You can't escape your destiny', I couldn't make it to IISc. I couldn't get an engineering course of my choice either. So, I was left with my last option, MBBS.

I was completely dejected and unwillingly joined GDMC, Dehradun. For an introvert like me, the idea of talking to patients and treating them was scary. I had doubts about whether I'll be able to talk to them with confidence as I was never a people person. So carrying my burdens of not getting into IISc and my doubts, I entered into my first year of MBBS.

First year had pre-clinical subjects, so my mind was relieved with the doubts I had. I studied, made a few friends but as my nature ensued, I didn't come into the limelight. Enter the second year and that's when the trouble began. Our clinical classes had begun and it was the time to interact with patients. It was not a surprise I had cold sweats and wet palms whenever my turn came. Eventually causing me to avoid them as much as I could. I knew this would impede me to learn the clinical aspects but my fears overpowered me at that time. So how did I overcome this?

First, I had to accept the fact that avoiding patients will not solve anything. I began my conversation by talking about them; who exactly are they? Where are they from? How is their life there? This helped me loosen up and led me to ask them clinical questions as well. I didn't realize it at that time, but it also helped me to talk to random people outside my college life. This made me realize that *I actually enjoy talking to people.*

By the end of third year, I became very comfortable talking and broke my shell. I fondly remember my PSM professional exam, where I had to visit a family. I talked to a very affable young lady and her adorable kids. Talking to the lady made me realize their struggles in real-time and gave me a new perspective on life. I realized how life can be nurtured in a dingy, unlit room.

Most importantly, I realized the privileges I have, which otherwise felt trifling. The ease with which I can access electricity, water, and food. The freedom to go wherever I wish to. The freedom to study. The freedom to have my own independent life. I can recall the lady's face beaming at me when I was talking to my examiner. To me, it was just average English, but for her, I was a model of a modern, educated woman who can change the world. At the time of leaving, she held my hand and said 'You sounded so amazing!'. This incident gave me the confidence I needed all this time.

Pursuing MBBS has made me more confident, outgoing, and humble. I am eager to go further down this path and see aspects of myself that I can't otherwise. Though this path can be tiring, arduous at times, I am ready to face the challenges, treat people and somewhere down the line, change myself. So reader, if you want to become a doctor, but are apprehensive because of the stress and violence around it? I'd say, go for it. Face them and become a better person. What's better than the opinion of an introverted doctor (to-be)?

Reshma Rajendran

Determined, reliable and helpful are the best words to describe and introduce Dr. Reshma Rajendran, an intern doctor. Driven by passion, she takes pride in volunteering and creating awareness about many burning issues through the student organizations that she is a part of. She revels in taking part in medical concept-based quizzes and other competitions, having won several on a state and national level.

Being a creative individual, she has always had a knack for writing, be it anything ranging from stories to essays. What sets her apart is her sincerity and dedication in whatever she strives to achieve. She is always on the lookout for opportunities to grow and learn as a person.

In her spare time, she enjoys writing and traveling. Taking the great Robin Cook as her inspiration, she hopes to write a captivating novel one day.

CHAPTER 35

From Dusk Till Dawn And Beyond

Through all walks of life, we encounter doctors. The unsung heroes at times, but they never fail to deliver. Their commitment goes far beyond a single day. I am undoubtedly proud to be in the process of becoming one.

I can recollect something that happened to me that very strongly imprinted on me as a young child. For around a month in the 2nd grade, I was admitted to the children's hospital. I had just returned to the United States after a nice 3-month long vacation at my grandparents' place in India. Unfortunately, I had contracted typhoid fever there and it was diagnosed only once we came back. As a kid at the time, I was oblivious to the big picture while admitted to the hospital. I enjoyed the books they gave me to read, the talks with kind nurses, getting to watch my favorite tv shows whenever I pleased, and eating a nice variety of meals every day. The part I dreaded the most would be receiving a couple of injections daily for blood tests and other laboratory investigations. I despised the pain it caused. My then-pediatrician had contacted us to check up on me. She suggested a topical numbing cream which, at that time I simply knew as something which stopped the pain. I was ecstatic after that. I began to see doctors in a new light. I saw how they tried to do their best to reduce our pain and treat the diseases to the best of their ability. That was one of my initial experiences with a doctor which to this very day I can recollect as a priceless memory.

Life truly is a miracle and I have experienced that feeling which manifested several times during my clinical postings. My first experience was getting to see a live birth. I was spellbound during the phenomenon. I saw how much the human body is capable of and how miraculous the process was. Seeing the pain that the mother was in which was quickly replaced by joy and relief on seeing the little one and hearing the first cry of the baby are memories I will hold forever. I remember even going to the extent of jokingly naming the little boy Arav with my friends. That is the profession of a doctor, miracles filled to the brim and memories for life.

There will be a countless number of times family and friends will consult you on various health issues they may be facing. At first, it is puzzling because you may not know the answers or how to diagnose at the time- probably being just a first-year medical student. However, you do want to help them and try your best to do so. I have been in such a position too. It's alright if you don't know, being empathic goes a long way. Sometimes the least you could do to help is be a shoulder to lean on and a pair of ears to listen to what is going on in their mind. That would help to an extent. But as the years go by and such questions are asked to you, you can help them and that's the best feeling ever. That is a perfect measure of your growth and tremendous increase in your knowledge.

Such joyous times are there but not without the accompaniment of struggles. Questions like- *is it really worth it? Can I do it?* -flood one's mind during crucial times such as exams. The stress and self-doubt may tower over you and it may even lead up to thoughts of regretting taking up the course. I learned it's important to believe in oneself. Being determined is a must as in the end it will all be worth it. So many individuals are living proof of that.

The COVID-19 pandemic brought the world to a standstill. No one saw it coming. The monotony of normal day to day life was replaced by numerous changes. Most people were confined to their homes with a lot of time on their hands. I was one of them too. I grew as a person drastically and learned so much. Most importantly, I took up opportunities to step out of my comfort zone and shine in places I never could imagine myself before. Ranging from public speaking to many competitions, the pandemic brought out the best in me. I'm sure many people could relax and get to spend more time with their families and even rediscover a forgotten hobby. This wasn't the case for doctors though. Doctors always bring their A-game but this was taking it to the next level. It was more like them as Avengers against the virus as Thanos. I can't think of a better way to put it. Their workload increased tremendously, they were at risk of infection and they couldn't be with their families. None of this affected them. They were happy to do their best to help. All across the globe, doctors were the saviors. They were truly put to the test in this pandemic and they didn't disappoint. They were committed to delivering and providing the necessary care for patients.

If you're a medical aspirant reading this, don't lose hope, believe in yourself, and go after your dreams. That's all it takes. Someday you will be someone's inspiration. Doctors are ever ready to take on any obstacle in their path. It is not an obligation, it's their choice and it's their passion. They will always be there, from dusk till dawn and beyond.

Shreya Datta

A true geek girl,the most familiar place to find Shreya is curled up in an invisible nook,totally immersed in the fantasy world of books and magical places.Those rare moments when she isn't lost in the wilderness of the moors or in the dangerous waves of stormy oceans,she strives to keep up with her separate identity as a first year medical student.A free spirit at heart with an introvert's quirky sense of humor,Shreya hopes to share her imaginary world of dreams and fantasies with the rest of the world one day.

Changes

If you ask my mom, she would promptly declare her incredulity and wonder at the solid reality of her daughter preparing to become a doctor in the future. If you consult her extensive, labyrinthine memory then I used to be one of those fussy, hypochondriac types of kids who spent hours fretting in front of the mirror, attempting to find out if I had any minuscule cut or scratch on my body. My unexplained childhood fear of injuries and the sudden attacks of fainting spells at the sight of blood quite worried my mother, you see. For her subdued, hidden hopes of visualizing her little girl in a white apron with a stethoscope around her neck were unknowingly marred by my paranoid inquiries if an accidental bumping of my head signifies my untimely demise.

Thankfully, I outgrew these silly habits just like a set of old clothes; but one thing remained unchanged-my purposeful, almost cruelly negligent attitude towards my mom's dreams for me. In fact, I was stubbornly dead-set against that prospect (true to my Taurian nature) as a thousand excuses cropped up in my head, discouraging me at every step. Sometimes, it would be- "I'm not talented enough", at other times it would be, "I lack the patience and determination to push myself through this whole arduous journey." And thus, time ticked on, with me, a happy-go-lucky teenager merrily skipping towards a foggy and uncertain future. Until tragedy struck.

Right now as I'm penning down these words, surprise hits me, accompanied by a dull ache, like the confusing pain of something hurting deep inside your chest in an unknown location, making it all the more difficult for you to draw each successive breath. Like in the aftermath of a ravenous storm, leaving behind only destruction and shattered dreams as the testimony to its awful presence. And I'm the unlucky survivor, drowning in the shuddering solitude of death and the ashes of unfulfilled desires. The suddenness of it all is what renders it all the more heart-wrenching; with no prior warning or premonition, tragedy makes her move, skilfully disguising her maleficent design of wreaking havoc on your life. For me, I clearly remember that day; it was sunny, almost painfully bright while the whole city was gearing up for the Christmas season of merry-making and cheerfulness. That's when the phone call came. A few staccato words choked out through a veil of emotions.

"It's your grandmother. She's dying. From terminal cancer."

They hit me like a shotgun, sadistically wringing out every ounce of blood from my body. The initial disbelief was followed by a stunned silence lasting for an eternity. Those moments remain hazily etched in my memory, only a few vivid flashes- my mother's sobbing face, dad's crestfallen look, and pathetic attempts at pacifying her. That smiling woman whose arms protected me throughout my childhood from the bedside monsters and ghosts; that woman who patiently endured all my tantrums and mischief while lulling me to sleep every night and now she is going to abandon me? Just like that? I was sorely tempted to dismiss the whole incident as a cruel joke, a simple fib and my immature mind tried its best to ingrain that silly idea into my whole being. My foolish hopes of maintaining my childhood castle by valiantly rejecting the sordid reality caused a lot of discord in the accompanying few months as my shameful journey of grappling with denial and acceptance began. It started with negligence towards my surroundings till it reached the situation where I drew a blank whenever someone talked to me; a never-ending series of nightmares haunted me the moment I closed my eyes and it finally climaxed when I flatly refused to go and visit her on her deathbed. My courage failed me with each passing moment as the cruel claws of reality pried open the flimsy shields I had built around myself and I was dragged down, screaming, crying, and sobbing, to visit her. From the moment I laid my eyes on that frail body, fighting for every single breath, a mere remnant of that beautiful person it used to be, my world came crashing down for a second time. But this time it was louder, more painful compared to the cloying silence of the first time. That was my first encounter with death. Or should I say the painfully slow and inevitable descent down towards oblivion? And the mercy of a swift and peaceful end was also denied. Rather, it was a whole conglomeration of despair and unbearable agony for both parties. We could only watch on helplessly, tightly clutching her during those moments when she writhed about wildly in horrendous physical pain. Eventually, however, we had to return and my last memory was bidding her goodbye with the final kiss, hot with my tears of regret and the burning sting of irreplaceable loss. But through that destruction of my old world bloomed a new hope, fragile with indecision yet firm with my determination to achieve it. And at that moment I vowed that whatever may come, even if I have to bend heaven and raise hell, I will become a doctor.

A reawakening at the age of 16, as I finally freed myself from the invisible shackles holding me back all this time to step out into a newfound clarity. I wanted to bring back the stolen smiles to sick people and lose myself in the service of others. And it took death and heartache to teach me about the frailty of human beings and the lesson was so harsh that it uprooted all my previous perceptions about life and instead sowed the seeds of living to save lives. And even though I've barely started on this lifelong journey, I am confident of facing all difficulties ahead with optimism and hope. And this concludes this unbelievable tale of the transformation of a little cry-baby who was scared of blood to that of a young girl enthusiastically endeavoring to dissect cadavers. So enthusiastic at times that her classmates marvel at her apparent lack of a gag reflex in the presence of the sickly stench of the preserving fluids. I guess this is why people say change is the only constant element in this fickle and brief life.

Pragya Chand

An unconventional third professional medical student who finds solace in books and poetry.Both Robbins and Oscar Wilde render her equally awestruck,while medicine is her passion,literature is her raison d'être.Being the current AMSA head for her institution,She is a visionary celebrating her amalgamated love for music and medicine.Can often be seen outside the library with her book stack vibing to John Mayer and James Bay whilst completely engrossed in the cosmogyral of her thoughts.This young lady is a staunch believer in the grandiosity of life and a devotee of medicine.She aims to specialize in Cardiology and has a vocation for oration which she often exercises in MUN conferences.The concept of holistic treatment of both mind and matter inspires her and her mind palace is her abditory of all-things-delightful.Certified aesthete,she-flaneur and a philocalist,the woman swears by her dynamic playlist and believes in leading The Jedi Life!However,the seemingly quiet hedonist blooms into a loquacious lass once strum to her frequency.

CHAPTER 37

The Metanoia

Friedrich Nietzche noticed that Autumn is more the season of the soul than of nature while F. Scott Fitzgerald believed that life starts all over again when it gets crisp in the fall. A thinker once said, "October is about trees revealing the colors they've hidden all year, people have an October as well."

There has always been this preposterous commitment of humans with the act of "falling", be it falling apart or falling together. The mellow tones of rust orange or the crisp sound of leaves crackling under you on a pavement while you are headed to the nearest coffee shop, the undeniable beauty of fall has been romanticized since time immemorial.

Amidst the Pandemic and the inevitable repercussions it brought along, Sapiens have taken all the hits in a stride, and slowly, but steadily evolved for their betterment. Science stands witness to this remarkable ability of adaptability and, to eliminate all the queries regarding its validity, concrete evidence exists for your understanding.

The first month of the infamous worldwide quarantine was equally detested by the multitude from all continents. However, the gusto with which we adapted to this new normal is commendable. The changing family dynamic, the constant hindrance in routine practices, and the trauma associated with it tunneled its way to an irrevocable outcome. Sapiens have yet again proven to be elite by thriving in such dysphoric situations and normalizing, what seemed so reprehensible, to be a new reality.*"Wabi-Sabi",* a beautiful Japanese word, translates to -the beauty and appreciation of things imperfect and impermanent; accepting the flow of life.

Needless to say, none of us were prepared for such an enormous trauma on the face of humanity and civilization. COVID-19 has left no soul untouched and the drive with which we are rising above it is no less than a miracle. The Internet has proven to be an asset in such times, nearly every business has been conducted online and kept the ship of the economy from drowning. But it also has stunted our ability to reason and amplifies our dependence on gizmos and gadgets. The amount of useless news that the media has been feeding us is rather ridiculous.

A strict self-imposed filter should be employed to preserve our mental health and sanity status (if that makes sense). Even the foremost rule of disaster management instructs you to help yourself before being a probable candidate for others. You cannot possibly pour from an empty glass; hence, self-care should be prioritized over half-hearted community service. Once you feel physically, emotionally, and spiritually stable make sure you become an ally to the distressed and assist them. I Must conclude by quoting my eternal favorite, John Keats:

"Of noble natures, of the gloomy days, of all the unhealthy and o'er-darkn'd ways

Rich with a sprinkling of fair musk-rose blooms, and such too is the grandeur of dooms

We have imagined for the mighty dead,

An endless fountain of immortal drink, pouring unto us from the heaven's brink."

END OF VOLUME-1

DIVE INTO MORE SUCH STORIES IN
VOLUME-2 OF WORLD THROUGH A STETHOSCOPE

Acknowledgment

"No one can whistle a symphony. It takes a whole orchestra to play it."
- H.E. Luccock

The establishment of this anthology book, Sept 2020, has been an endeavour that could not have been materialised without the support, loyalty, and contributions of numerous individuals. I want to express our deep appreciation to all those who have made a substantial contribution to making this project a reality. It began as a simple effort to lend a voice to the voiceless, became much more. The metamorphosis of World through a Stethoscope over last 3 years has been truly astonishing.

First and foremost, I'd like to thank the **Core Team**, without whom, the book won't have come to life. **Navneet Mishra**, the Creative Head, the steadfast cornerstone, whose creative genius, artistic insight, and organizational expertise have not only enhanced the visual elements of the book, encompassing the cover design and social media presence, but also guaranteed the maintenance of high standard. **Manali Despande**, the face behind iconic half heart and half stethoscope trademark WTS emblem, has given astounding spin to visual facets with her skills. **Muskaan Shah**, the Associate Editorial head, who has instilled life and vigor into the words on these pages. **Rushikesh Ghorband** and **Ruthik Nahar**, who played a major role during the initial inception and execution of this idea.

I would like to convey my thanks to the accomplished authors whose writings enrich the pages of this anthology. These tales are sure to kindle abundant inspiration. Your inventive skills and unwavering passion have animated the words within these pages, and we deeply respect your artistic expertise.

Our gratitude extends to the families and friends of the contributors, who provided support, encouragement, and understanding during the creative process.

I would also like to express our appreciation to the organizations, who helped us increase our outreach - **Aspire, AMSA, Switch India, Squad Research and Medicine, Being Medic** and **Medical Students' Syncytium**.

Last but not least, I would like to thank my parents - **Dnyandeo Shelar** and **Yogita Shelar**, my younger brother - **Omkar Shelar**, and close friends, who were constant sources of strength, encouragement and resilience, through various ups and downs, without whom, this book wouldn't have been possible. The families and confidants of our authors, are the unsung heroes of this narrative, for you have provided the foundation upon which your children have built their noble careers.

Last but not least, we would like to extend our gratitude to our community of healthcare professionals, the unsung heroes who provide compassion and care, saving lives and spreading hope with every act of dedication.

Your contributions have made this book a reality, and I hope it brings joy and inspiration to readers for years to come. I believe that this anthology will not only be a valuable resource for those considering a career in healthcare, but it will also provide insight and inspiration for those already working in the field.

Thank you.

Founder and CEO,

Dr Tejas Shelar

WTS Logo Decoded

The following logo has been conceptualised and designed by **Dr Tejas Shelar** and **Navneet Mishra.**

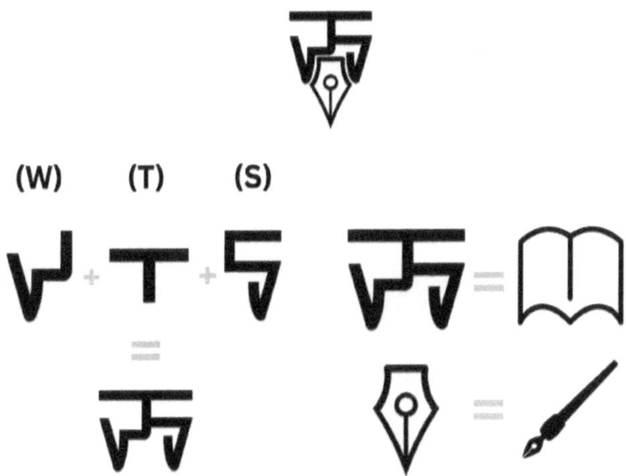

The following emblem has been conceptualised and designed by **Manali Deshpande.**

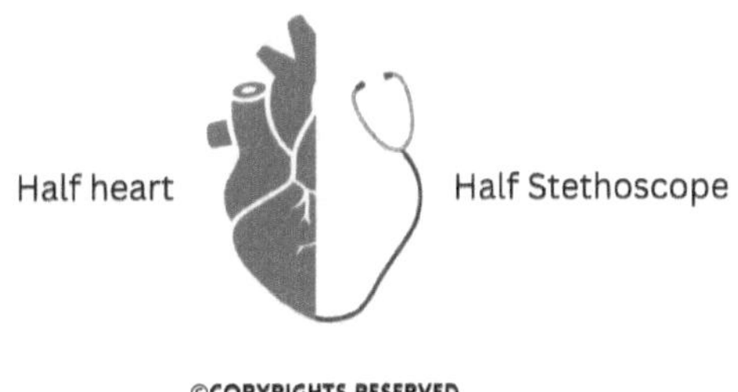

Contact Us

World through a Stethoscope

Medical journey and experiences

An anthology, by medical professionals

Dr. Tejas

We have more opportunities coming up for, healthcare professionals in publishing realm, because we believe,

"Wherever we originate, whoever we are, and wherever we may be headed, our lives are woven from stories, and it's stories that will endure as our lasting legacy."

Follow us on our Socials   :

Instagram : @worldthroughastethoscope

LinkedIn : @worldthroughastethoscope

Facebook : @worldthroughastethoscope

Contact us :

Email ID : worldthroughastethoscope@gmail.com

Website : thewtsworld.com